Heavenly Highs

by Peter Stafford

RONIN PUBLISHING
BERKELEY, CA
WWW.RONINPUB.COM

Heavenly Highs

Published by
Ronin Publishing, Inc.
PO Box 22900
Oakland, CA 94609
www.roninpub.com

Technical Editor:	Jeremy Bigwood
Reconfiguration Editor:	Beverly Potter
Molecular Diagrams:	Alexander Shulgin
Cover & Interior Design:	Beverly Potter
Cover Painting:	Laurence Cherniak Laurence@Cherniak.com

Fonts: Venis family by Chank; Polynesian Tourist by Astigmatic; Zoomorphica by David D. Nalle of Scriptorium; MesoDeko, MayaDay Nmaes, AztecDaySigns,MayaMonthGlyphs by Deniart Systems; and Palatino by Apple and Type Solutions.

Library of Congress Card Number: 2005900582

Distributed to the book trade by **Publishers Group West**

Printed in the United States by **United Graphics**

Material derived from Chapters Five - Eight of *Psychedelics Encyclopedia*, Third Expanded Edition

Heavenly Highs

BOOKS BY PETER STAFFORD

Psychedelics
Magic Mushrooms
Psychedelics Encyclopedia
LSD—The Problem-Solving Psychedelic
co-authored with Bonnie Golightly
Psychedelic Baby Reaches Puberty

Table of Contents

Introduction

he heavenly plants discussed in this book have a colorfully romantic history, botany and chemistry. And each has shown itself capable of inducing powerful conscious-expanding and spirit-arousing effects.

The most popular entheogens are LSD, magic mushrooms, marijuana, and a host of substances related to both peyote and Ecstasy, which I've discussed in considerable detail in *Psychedelics Encyclopedia*, *Psychedelics* and *Magic Mushrooms*. In *Heavenly Highs* we have a grab-bag of historically significant mind-changers whose roots and influences have greatly affected the contemporary and classic entheogenic picture.

The first wave of the entheogenic invasion, as some have called it, occurred via the agency of these heavenly plant substances. This was then followed in the late 18th and early 19th century by growing interest in peyote and mescaline. Albert

Hofmann ushered in the third entheogenic wave with his discovery of the psychoactivity of LSD in 1943.

After that incursion cresting in the 1960s, and a considerable ebbing, the psilocybian mushrooms popularized by R. Gordon Wasson were promulgated throughout society—what with the identifiability and gentleness of psychoactive fungi. And then in the mid-1980s, we saw a fifth wave washing over us with the popularity of MDMA (Ecstasy).

The influence of psychoactives is the sum of effects that are greatly shaped by intentionality and half a dozen other major factors, especially in the areas of creativity, religion, and psychotherapy. This is illustrated quite clearly in stories to be told ahead. Fasten your seatbelts! A wild, absorbing trip is about to come!

—Peter Stafford

1
Psychedelic Snuffs

he first European observation of
entheogenics use in the New World
involved *cohoba* snuff, a powerful
mind-alterer made from seeds of the
yopo tree, *Anadenanthera peregrina*. The main
psychoactive components are DMT (N,N-dimethyl-
tryptamine) and 5-methoxy-DMT. These and related compounds are present in dozens of other
trees, vines, grasses, shrubs—even in mushrooms—
and in the "dream fish" and in the shoulder glands
of a frog called *Bufo giganticus*, which is native to a
southwestern U.S. desert.

This particular compound cluster exhibits a
two-ring, "open-chained," indolic chemical structure, and in contrast to other entheogens it is all
but inactive when taken orally unless accompanied
by specific other compounds. Short-acting
tryptamines are closely related to neurotransmitters such as bufotenine, to MDA—a major botanical
source of the snuffs belongs to the nutmeg family,

Cohoba snuff is made from the seeds of the Anadananthera perigrina tree.

to tryptophan, which is an essential amino acid produced in human digestion of proteins, and to psilocybin and psilocin, which are tryptamines of longer duration. DMT, the simplest member, occurs normally in the blood, brain and, in higher concentrations, in cerebrospinal fluid.

DMT, DET (N, N-diethyltryptamine) and DPT (N, N-dipropyltryptamine) are the compounds in this cluster that have been manufactured and distributed most over the last half century. Compared with psychedelics like LSD and psilocybin, use of these tryptamines has been limited and irregular. Yet they constitute a psychedelic grouping of great importance in the United States and elsewhere.

New World Native Use

The Spanish friar Ramon Paul, who accompanied Columbus on his second voyage to the New World, was the first to record native use of entheogenics when he saw the Taino Indians of what is now called Haiti snorting "kohhobba" to communicate with the spirit world. The snuff was made of seeds from the foot-long pods of a mimosa-like tree that grows wild only in South America. By the time of

Columbus' second voyage, the natives of the West Indies probably found it easier to plant the trees than to maintain communication with the mainland for their source of supply.

Indians along the Rio Guaviaro in Colombia as far back as 1560 were accustomed to taking *Yopa*—"a seed or pip of a tree"—together with tobacco, becoming "drowsy while the devil, in their dreams, shows them all the vanities and corruptions he wishes them to see and which they take to be true revelations in which they believe, even if told they will die."

A Jesuit wrote in 1741 about *cohoba* use by the Otomac Indians of the Orinoco region between Colombia and Venezuela. Referring to it as an "abominable habit", the priest described the Indians as intoxicating themselves through the nostrils "with certain malignant powders which they call Yupa, which takes away their reason and they will furiously take up arms". Describing details of the snuff's preparation, including addition of lime from snail shells, he reported that before a battle, the Indians would "throw themselves into a frenzy with Yupa, wound themselves and, full of blood and rage, go forth to battle like rabid jaguars".

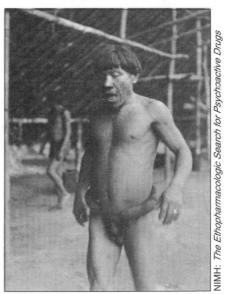

Intoxicated native

NIMH: *The Ethopharmacologic Search for Psychoactive Drugs*

Modern Native Use

Richard Schultes and Albert Hofmann write in *Plants of the Gods* that *Virola* snuff is used among many groups in Amazonian Colombia and Venezuela, the Rio Negro, and other areas of the western Amazon of Brazil. The southernmost locality of its known use is among the Paumare Indians of the Rio Purus in the southwestern Amazon of Brazil. In Colombia, use is usually restricted to shamans, who employ this snuff "ritualistically for diagnosis and treatment of disease, prophecy, divination, and other magico-religious purposes."

Among other tribes, especially those known collectively as the Waika, *epena* may be used individually as well as ceremonially by any male over the age of thirteen or fourteen. Amounts as large as two to three teaspoons are blown into the nostrils through long tubes. Ingestion of large doses is repeated regularly over a two- to three-day period during at least one annual ceremony.

Natives often use snuffing daily. In Colombia and Venezuela, Hoffer and Osmond write that the *yopo*-snuffing habit "was carried on by whole populations. The intoxication produced convulsive movements and distortions of face and body muscles, then a desire to dance and finally an inability to control their limbs. Then a violent madness or deep sleep overtook the user. Then they developed stupor."

Some Indian tribes, particularly those among the Waikas, use psychoactive snuffs in what Schultes and Hofmann refer to as frighteningly excessive amounts. They reported that *Virola* resins with a DMT and 5-methoxy-DMT content as high as 11 percent are routinely ingested in quantities as large as two or three teaspoonfuls.

Leaves of the Angel of Death

"Leaves of the Angel of Death" or *bolek-hena* is the name for one such snuff derived from the *Justicia pectoralis* variety *stenophylla* of the family Acanthaceae. This red-flowered herb enjoys a considerable popularity among the Waikas. Among these peoples, three *curanderos* have died from using this potent snuff which seems to contain fairly large amounts of tryptamines in the dried and powdered leaves. Often it is an adulterant of snuffs made from the red bark resin of several species of *Virola*.

—William Emboden

There is no unequivocal archeological evidence showing ancient use of *cohoba* or *epena* snuffs. However, widespread shamanic use and the considerable mythology associated with both snuffs suggest that such traditions go far into the past. Snuffing artifacts have been found all over South America, though these implements may have been used for tobacco.

More recently, the Mashco Indians of northern Argentina were reported to smoke and sniff a preparation from *Anadenanthera colubrina* seeds, confirming early Spanish reports of snuffs being made of this species, commonly known as *vilca*. According to one such account from 1571, Incan medicine men made prophecies through inebriation brought about by drinking *chicha* reinforced with *vilca*. *A. colubrina* snuff has since been assayed as having essentially the same psychoactive makeup as *cohoba* and *epena* snuffs.

Goncalves deLima, a Brazilian ethnobotanist and chemist, extracted an alkaloid in 1946 from roots of *Mimosa hostilis*, another member of the pea family, which has been used by natives of eastern Brazil to prepare a potent psychoactive drink. He named this "nigerine." Later it was found to be identical to DMT, first synthesized in 1931 by British chemist Richard Manske.

Effects of Cohoba and Epena Snuffs

Observing Guahibo Indians in the mid-nineteenth century, Richard Spruce remarked that using *cohoba* snuff eliminated hunger and thirst because "one feels so good" and compared the inebriation to that from Fly Agarics. The Catauixi used the snuff when they were about to go on a hunt in order to render themselves more alert. Schultes and Hofmann reported that snuff from the *yopo* tree is sometimes taken as a daily stimulant among the Guahibo. "But it is more commonly employed by *payes*—medicine men—to induce trances and visions and communicate with the *hekula* spirits; to prophesy or divine; to protect the tribe against epidemics of sickness; to make hunters and even their dogs more alert."

Indians under the effects of this *Virola* resin "characteristically have faraway dreamlike expressions that are, of course, due to the active principles of the drug, but which the natives believe are associated with the temporary absence of the shamans' souls as they travel to distant places. The chants during the incessant dancing performed by shamans may at times reflect conversations with spirit forces. This transportation of the soul to other realms represents to the Waika one of the most significant values of the effects of this hallucinogen."

Emboden adds a fascinating comment on the striking tribal differences in visions produced by *epena*. He said that among the Witotos, microscopia, or seeing things and people miniaturized, is a characteristic of the *Virola* syndrome;

Mimosa hostilis

while for the Waika macroscopia is a part of the visionary experience. This is probably conditioned in part by the tryptamines and in part by cultural background. "Macroscopia is inextricable from the Waika concepts of *hikura*, the spirit who dwells in the *Virola* tree."

Botanical Sources

William Safford determined in 1916 that the psycho-active principles of *cohoba* snuff did not come from especially powerful tobacco, as was generally thought at the time, but from the beans of *Anadenanthera peregrina*—a member of the pea family, formerly placed in the genus of *Piptadenia,* then *Mimosa and Acacia.*

The Brazilian botanist Ducke identified a second kind of psychoactive snuff as coming from a an-other species in 1938. He reported that Indians of the upper Rio Negro employed leaves of *Virola*

theiodora and *Virola cuspidata* in making a powder
they called *parica*. Ducke was wrong about the
leaves; the Indians used sap from the inner bark. By
pinpointing a species other than the leguminous
trees from which *cohoba* is derived, however, Ducke
prompted further investigations into plant
psychoactivity where no nonnative had previously
thought to look.

The brownish snuff described by Ducke was
known as *yakee* among the Punave, as *yato* among
the Kuripako and as *epena* among the Waika tribes.
His detailed account described its botany, preparation and shamanistic use by the Barasana, Makuna,
Tukano, Kaluyare, Puhave and other tribes in eastern Colombia. *V. calophylla* and *V. calophylloidea*
were then considered the main entheogenic species
in use, but *V. theiodora* has since come to be recog-
nized as the most prevalent and highly prized.

Anadenanthera Peregrina

This source of the snuff, known as *yopo*, from the
South American Orinoco basin, was noticed by the
time of Columbus' second trip to The New World
in 1506. It's from a tree that grows to 60 feet, with
perhaps a 2 foot diameter. The inner bark is psychoactive.

Anadenanthera peregrina grows throughout the
Caribbean, and in Brazil, Columbia, Guyana, Para-
guay, Suriname and Venezuela. The pods, generally
gathered between January and February, are flat
and contain 3-10 seeds, which are glossy black and
round in appearance.

Another growing area for *Anadenanthera* is
slightly smaller and centers in northern Argentina,
where the seed snuff is known as *cebil*. Three

species native to southern Peru and Bolivia—*A. macrocarpa, A. excelsa* and *A. colubrina*—are the source of *vilca* and *huilca*. All four *Anadenanthera* species seem to be used in making snuffs, usually without other plant additives.

Tryptamine Content

The active principles in *Anadenanthera* and *Virola* snuffs are indolic alkaloids—either "open-chained" or "closed-ring" tryptamines. The "open-chained" group however includes DMT and 5-methoxy-DMT, as well as bufotenine, which appears to be non-psychoactive. DMT predominates in the species *Virola calophylla*, but in other species the greatest psychic contribution comes from the very short-acting 5-methoxy-DMT.

Trace amounts of the "open-chained" DMT-N-oxide and 5-hydroxy-DMT-N-oxide, as well as "closed-ring" tryptamines 2-methyl- and 1,2-di-methyl-7-methoxytetrahydro-β-carboline, are present in both *Anadenanthera* and *Virola* snuffs, adding somewhat to their effects. *Virolas* also contain small quantities of 6-methoxy-DMT and monoethyltryptamine.

Stomberg isolated 5-methoxy-DMT from seeds of *A. peregrina*. DMT, DMT-N-oxide and 5-hydroxy-DMT-N-oxide were also found in *A. peregrina*. Additional components contributing to psychoactivity have also been identified. These appear in about the same proportions in the *Virola* species used to make *parica*. However, a Waika snuff made from *V. theiodora* resin has an unusually high alkaloid content of up to 11 percent, consisting mainly of 5-methoxy-DMT (8 percent) and substantial amounts of DMT.

This 5-methoxy-DMT compound had already been observed in toads and even in a "dream fish"— *Kyphosus fuscus*—found off Norfolk Island in the South Pacific. In order to test the claim by inhabitants that this fish produces "nightmares," Joe Roberts, a photographer for *National Geographic,* broiled and ate some. The next morning, he reported his experience to have been "pure science fiction". He said that he saw a new kind of car, monuments to mark humanity's first trip into space and so on. A skeptical writer with him admitted, "I ate a dream fish supper myself. I found it tasty, but strong flavored, like mackerel. I told myself not to dream. But no. I dreamed I was at a party where everybody was nude and the band played, 'Yes, We Have No Pajamas!"

How Snuff is Snorted

Snuff is harsh and burns the nose lining, which makes it difficult to inhale enough of a dosage. Traditionally natives used a "snorter" to inhale, which has a tube going from the mouth of each person to the nose of the other. Rather than snorting, the device is loaded and then one person "blows" the snuff into the other's nose, which

NIMH: *The Ethopharmacologic Search for Psychoactive Drugs*

Native snuff snorting tubes

thrusts a large amount deep into the nasal cavity. The person getting the first hit must immediately blow a dose into the other person's nose before falling into the trance. These powerful snuffs blown into the upper nasal passages, often into the sinuses, induce violent fits of sneezing followed by profound hallucinations.

Smoking Snuff

Many people find snorting snuff to be unpleasant, causing acute distress to the nasal passages. To get around this problem people have experimented with grinding and smoking the seeds rather than snort-ing them. The approach is effec-

NIMH: *The Ethopharmacologic Search for Psychoactive Drugs*

An Indian blows snuff into his friend's nose.

tive. However, the smoke from the seeds leaves a peculiar, unpleasant aftertaste. One-third to one-half of a toasted ground seed is plenty to observe the effects. There is often a strong sensation of muscle tension and bodily tightness. This is accompanied by strong visual distortions and color changes. When the physical energy subsides, the mental effects are more pronounced with deep states of thought likened to the late stages of a mescaline experience.

Some people have experimented with smoking a combination of *Anadenanthera colubrina* and *Salvia divinorum*. The mixture is reported to be potent and more profound and pleasant than either smoked separately. It seems to contain a lot of the *Salvia* weirdness. The somatic effects are profound making the user want to move and dance.

Preparation

German explorer and naturalist Baron Alexander von Humboldt identified the *yopo* tree botanically in 1801. While collecting flora near the Orinoco River, he watched the Maypure Indians prepare *cohoba* snuff by breaking the pods, moistening them and allowing them to ferment. When the pods turned black, they were kneaded with cassava meal and lime from snails into small cakes, which were eventually powdered. Humboldt noted, "It is not to be believed that the pods are the chief cause of the effects of the snuff. These effects are due to the freshly calcinated lime." The lime, however, in fact adds nothing to the snuff's psychoactivity.

Fifty years later, a British explorer and naturalist, Richard Spruce, made detailed observations of the preparation and use of *yopo* among the Guahlbo of the Orinoco basin, commenting that it was used by all the tribes of the upper tributaries. He purchased equipment consisting of a grinder, platter, wooden spatula, a container made from the leg bone of a jaguar and a Y-

Natives preparing snuff

NIMH: *The Ethopharmacologic Search for Psychoactive Drugs*

shaped snuffing tube for preparing and snorting their *niopo* seeds. The seeds and pods he collected in 1851 for chemical studies weren't analyzed, however, until 1977.

German anthropologist Theodor Koch-Grunberg described another psychoactive snuff in 1909, which was prepared from a tree bark and inhaled during ritualistic cures by the Yekwanas at the headwaters of the Orinoco.

Magical Snuff

This is a magical snuff, exclusively used by witch doctors and prepared from the bark of a certain tree which, when pounded up, is boiled in a small earthenware pot, until all the water has evaporated and a sediment remains at the bottom of the pot. This sediment is toasted in the pot over a slight fire and is then finely powdered with the blade of a knife. Then the sorcerer blows a little of the powder through a reed into the air. Next, he snuffs, whilst, with the same reed, he absorbs the powder into each nostril successively. The *hakudufha* obviously has a strongly stimulating effect, for immediately the witch doctor begins singing and yelling wildly, all the while pitching the upper part of his body backwards and forwards.

—Theodor Koch-Grunberg

2

DMT

MT and 5-methoxy-DMT are entheogenic substances that naturally occur in many plants, most of which grow in the Amazon. These alkaloids can be manufactured synthetically—as separate compounds—which are then sold underground. Interestingly, DMT is also manufactured naturally in the human body,

The first recorded experiences of pure DMT took place when the pharmacologist Stephen Szara, who was Chief of the National Institute of Drug Abuse's biomedical research branch, injected himself and friends intramuscularly with this compound in 1957. He administered 75 mg. to himself.

The onset of the experience came within three to four minutes. Szara noted trembling, nausea, dilation of the pupils and an elevated blood pressure and pulse rate, accompanied by brilliantly colored oriental motifs and, later, "rapidly changing wonderful scenes". He became euphoric and said that his attention was so firmly bound to the visual phenomena that he was unable to describe them until the experience passed, some forty-five to sixty minutes after its start.

Szara established by further testing that intramuscular injection of 50 to 60 mg. of DMT brought about intense visual displays—with eyes open or closed—within five minutes. These reached peak effects within a quarter of an hour, diminishing and then disappearing totally within half an hour to one hour, at the longest, Subjects became catatonic or lost consciousness when given doses larger than 125 mg.

Albert Hofmann, who had by then synthesized LSD, soon thereafter produced a series of DMT analogs, but little attention was paid to this work until the mid-1960s.

The Terror Drug

Ironically, interest in DMT began to develop after an adverse experience with DMT. William Burroughs, author of *Naked Lunch* and *Junkie,* figured prominently in the beatnik movement. He journeyed in 1960 to Peru in search of *yage* and had experimented with stroboscopic machines to produce hallucinations.

Allen Ginsberg told Timothy Leary during the winter of 1960 that Burroughs "knows more about drugs than anyone alive" and urged him to initiate a correspondence. Burroughs' second letter to Leary was dated May 6, 1961.

Dear Dr. Leary:

I would like to sound a word of urgent warning with regard to the hallucinogen drugs with special reference to Dimethyl-tryptamine. I had obtained a supply of this drug synthesized by a chemist friend in London. My first impression was that it closely resembled psilocybin in its effects.

I had taken it perhaps ten times (this drug must be injected and the dose is about one grain [approximately 65 mg.] but I had been assured that there was a wide margin of safety) with results sometimes unpleasant but well under control and always interest-ing when the horrible experience occurred which I have recorded and submitted for publication in *Encounter* (a then-current magazine).

—William Burroughs

In *High Priest*, Leary recalls that he and his associ-ates studied Burroughs' letter, deciding to reserve judgment until after further experiments. "We had learned enough to know that set-and-setting deter-mined the reaction, not the drug. Bill Burroughs alias Doctor Benway had inadvertently taken an overdose (about 100 mg.) of DMT and was flung into a space-fiction paranoia."

Jeremy Bigwood and Jonathan Ott, writing in *Head* magazine, noted that during his period of terror Burroughs had been "gulping down some of his 'metabolic regulator' apomorphine as an anti-dote."

Bigwood and Ott noted that were it not for Timothy Leary, Richard Alpert, and Ralph Metzner, the terror drug would have been excluded from the Psychedelic Age. Although these three had heard nothing but negative reports about the effects of this compound, undaunted they decided to test the drug on themselves. They discovered that when one observes the rules of "set" and "setting," DMT produces a short but ecstatic experience.

The *Psychedelic Review* recorded a Leary experience of DMT where Ralph Metzner sat nearby taking notes, asking at regular intervals: "Where are you now?" In this collaborative article, Metzner's observations appear in a column opposite Leary's perceptions as recalled later. Immersed in the sight of giant, gold-encrusted, shimmering beetles, Leary said that he heard a voice off in the distance asking, "Where...are...you...now?"

Afterward, Leary proposed development of an "experiential typewriter" for recording such rapid, high-intensity experiences. Experimenters were to be trained in pressing keys, each of which represented a particular state of mind that could be recorded on a paper tape and later correlated with the passage of time. While a prototype for such a machine was attempted but never reached a functioning state. Leary and Metzner's article caused a wave of interest in DMT among many in the counterculture.

DPT and Speculations

Reports about DPT use began appearing in the late 1970s in the psychological literature, both in connection with therapy and in efforts to ease the anxieties of dying patients. This short-acting tryptamine, bearing a longer side-chain than that in DMT, induced entheogenic experiences of about three-and-a-half hours duration that often came to an abrupt ending, a feature that appealed to some therapists. Many patients reported having "peak experiences" under DPT. Some people who administered this compound felt, however, that LSD had more memorable results, even if more tiring due to its longer duration.

Terence McKenna, in noting that DMT occurs as a neurotransmitter in ordinary human metabolism, asked:

> Now isn't that interesting? That the most powerful and radical and alien of all these hallucinogens is the one most like—in fact, exactly like—what's in your own body? This is also a Catch 22 for the Establishment, 'cause it means we're all holding—all the time!

> Now it's known that DMT is at its highest concentration in cerebrospinal fluid between 3 and 4 am in most people. And that's the time of day when the deep REM sleep occurs, accompanied by deep dreaming

McKenna concludes that it looks like the chemistry of dream and the chemistry of the psychedelic experience are the same.

> I took this stuff to Tibetans. To the Amazon. I gave it to Tibetans. They said, 'This is the lesser lights, the lesser lights of the Bardo. You cannot go further into the Bardo, and return. This takes you as far as you can go.' When I gave it to shamans in the Amazon, they

said, 'It's strong. But these are the ancestors.
These are the spirits that we work with. These
are ancestor souls. We know this place.'"

In *DMT: The Spirit Molecule* Strassman says;

I was drawn to DMT because of its presence
in all of our bodies. Perhaps excessive DMT
production, coming from the mysterious pineal
gland, was involved in naturally occurring
'psychedelic' states. These might include birth,
death and near-death, psychosis, and mystical
experiences. Only later, while the study was
well underway, did I also begin considering
DMT's role in the 'alien abduction' experience.

Strassman's account includes excerpts from his
some 1,000 pages of bedside notes that he hoped
would provide a sense of the remarkable emotional,
psychological, and spiritual effects of this chemical.

Descriptions of the extensive variety of intense
experience that may result from sequential research
perhaps is best expressed by Henri Micheau. "How to
describe it!?" exclaims the French poet and painter,
speaking of the entheogenic
experience. "It would require
a picturesque style which I
do not possess, made up
surprises, of nonsense, of
sudden flashes, of bounds
and rebounds, an unstable
style, tobogganing and
prankish." Micheau was
writing about mescaline
experiences, but it applies
as well to DMT and the
harmalas.

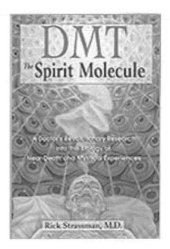

Cliff Pickover speculates in *DMT, Moses, and the Quest for Transcendence* that DMT in the pineal glands of Biblical prophets gave God to humanity and let ordinary humans perceive parallel universes. He goes on to wonder if it is possible that our brain is a filter and that the use of DMT is like slipping on infrared goggles, allowing us to perceive a valid reality that is inches away and all around us. Often DMT entities lack depth. Pickover questions if a higher-production of DMT in ancient people could influence artwork. "Is that part of the reason why cave paintings and Egyptian art are so two dimensional?" Pickover was emphatic in his statement that his taking DMT was the most profoundly moving experience of his "known live experience of this life on Earth".

Well-known psychedelic explorer James Kent, former editor of *Entheogen Review* and *Trip* magazine, emphasized that the visions produced by DMT are not solely elves and alien entities. They are a wide variety of archetypes, and "just plain-old whacked-out stoner shit creeps into the mix".

The really interesting thing for Kent about DMT experiences is not the elves (messengers) themselves, but what it is they are saying (the message). He says when you get to the heart of what the typical DMT message is, it is usually something about the environment or living systems or the vast plant consciousness that penetrates our world.

Anadenanthera

Anadenanthera peregrina grows naturally and is cultivated throughout about a tenth of South America. Its primary locale is described by Schultes and Hofmann as the plains or grasslands of the Orinoco basin of Colombia and Venezuela, in light forests in southern British Guiana (now known as Guyana), and in the Rio Branco area of the northern Amazonia of Brazil. It also appears in isolated savanna areas where it has been introduced by natives, notably the Rio Madeira region. *Anadenanthera peregrina* was also cultivated in the West Indies until the late 1800s.

Source of the first psychedelic observed in the New World.

D.V. Siva Sankar's enormous green book *LSD: A Total Study* lists eleven legumes that contain bufotenine and DMT. Of these, the second most widely used is *Mimosa hostilis.* Decoctions made from its root play a part in the ceremonies of the ancient Yurema cult of Brazil. The decoction is known as the "wine of Jurema."

William Emboden describes this "miraculous drink" as "a wondrous beverage that gives visions of the spirit world. Intended for priests, warriors, and strong young men, the infusion permits a glimpse into the world where rocks destroy the souls of the dead and the Thunderbird sends lightning from his head and runs about producing thunder. The Pankaruru Indians use a similar brew from the bark of *Mimosa verrucos* or the *caatinga* shrub under the name *Jurema branca*; it too contains N–N–DMT."

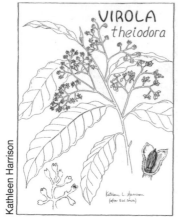

Kathleen Harrison

Psychoactive tryptamines are found in the inner bark of Virola theiodora.

Virolas

At least sixty species of the genus *Virola*, part of the *Myristiceae* (nutmeg) family, are known to exist in the New World, chiefly in the tropical regions of Central and South America. A dozen such species have been assayed as containing DMT-type alkaloids, but they are used for inducing visions and trances only around the western Amazon and in adjacent parts of the Orinoco basin. The most frequently used is *V. theiodora*. Others processed into psychoactive snuffs are *V. calophylla, V. calophylloides, V. elongata* and *V. cuspidata*. Resins of *V. sebifera* are smoked by some Venezuelan Indians. A few references to smoking have appeared in connection with other Virolas as well.

DMT-like compounds appear in the sap of the inner bark—not in the seeds or roots—of *Virolas*. The making of *epena* therefore involves stripping *Virolas* of their outer bark. An almost colorless liquid then exudes from the bark, quickly turning to blood red, which is the result of enzyme activity, and hardening into a shiny, gummy resin. The tryptamines and other indoles lose potency rapidly unless heated immediately. Natives scrape off the inner bark and heat it or boil it after soaking the bark for about twenty minutes in cold water. Once the psychoactive compounds are stabilized, the resin is usually made into a powder.

Amazing Botanical Knowledge

Indians who are familiar with *Virola* trees from the point of view of their hallucinogenic potency, exhibit uncanny knowledge of different "kinds" which to a botanist appear to be indistinguishable as to species. Before stripping the bark from a trunk, they are able to predict how long the exudate will take to turn red, whether it will be mild or peppery to the tongue when tasted, how long it will retain its potency when made into snuff, and many other hidden characteristics... there is no doubt about the Indian's expertness in recognizing these differences, for which he often has a terminology.

—Schultes and Hofmann

Plants of the Gods

Several bushes, vines, grasses and mushrooms also contain DMT and its chemical relatives. Leaves from Psychotria viridis, a bush belonging to the coffee family, and Banisteriopsis rusbyana, an ivy-like vine, are often added to the drink called yage made from the Amazonian "visionary vine".

Plants Containing DMT

There are about a thousand or so plants that contain significant amounts of N,N-dimethyltryptamine (DMT).

Virola Theiodora

Here, in the Cumala tree, we have another example of DMT occurring in a red resin in the inner bark of this slender tree, generally growing 25 to 75 feet

R. E. Schultes/ Harvard Botanical

Scraping the bark of Virola

high, found in the forests of the Amazon. The bark is brown but mottled by gray patches, and the pungent flowers appear singly or in clusters of up to ten. The leaves are oblong, and half the seed is coated orange-red.

Acacia longifolia

A native of Eastern Australia, this ever-green tree or shrub, which is branched with long, thin leaves, can grow to over 20 feet tall. It has an oblong fruit of about 2-1/2 inches, is a nitrogen-fixant for the ground and exhibits large, yellow stamens about as large as its leaves. Known as the "Golden Wattle", this hardy plant grows along creeks and swamps. It prefers full sun, and flowers between July and November. Its seeds appear in green pods.

Natives have used the leaves to kill fish because they contain hydrocyanic composites. The trunk bark, especially if picked in the winter, can contain up to 0.2% N,N-dimethyltryptamine. Traces of DMT are found in the leaves.

Acanthaceae justicia

The Waikas of the Orinoco headwaters in Venezuela use the dried and pulverized leaves of this showy tropical shrub that attains a height of about 3 feet. Sometimes called Brazilian Red Cloak or Red

Justicia, this plant was originally thought to be from Venezuela. It has stout stems and broad leaves. A Mexican variant—there are at least 420 species in the family—is known as the Shrimp Plant, since the array of arched rose-pink to salmon or pale yellow bracts surrounding its white flowers resemble a shrimp. It flowers in the summer, and is noted for attracting hummingbirds.

Desmanthus illinoenesis

The root bark of this North American perennial shrub contains approximately 0.34% DMT, which can be extracted by pounding the root so the bark splits and can be peeled. Known sometimes as the "Illinois Bundleflower" or the "Prairie Mimosa", it grows to about 3 feet high and has some 30-50 flowers per head. This weedy legume is found from the Rockies to the Appalachians and grows in moist or dry soil on river banks, thickets, glades, prairies and pastures.

Mimosa hostilis

The Brazilian ceremonial drink, *Vinho do Jurema*, is produced by cooking the stems and root bark of this bushy treelet for some 24 hours. There is about 1% DMT in the root bark.

Reed Canary Grass

Then there is this easily grown grass—*P. aruninacea,* which like most grasses spreads through runners. "This plant is easy to obtain", writes Mescalito Ted in an article about smokable dimethyltryptamine from organic sources, "looks almost identical to common lawn grass, has some of the highest concentrations of DMT, and is beyond easy to grow."

3
DMT Consumption
& Safety

here are serious safety concerns that anyone contemplating experimenting with DMT should pay close attention to. This amazing entheogen can be injected but it is more often smoked. It acts synergistically with LSD and other psychoactivators.

Injection

When DMT is injected, the onset of effects usually takes two to five minutes, which is the time required for the tryptamine to make its way to the brain. The user becomes ecstatic for ten to fifteen minutes, declining to normal states of mind over the next quarter to half hour. Injected DET displays a similar curve of effects but lasts about three hours. DPT has about the same duration as DET but ends more abruptly.

Smoking Synthetic DMT

DMT comes in a crystalline form as an off-white to brownish or yellowish powder. The mechanics of loading and smoking, which is similar to freebasing, can be tricky. A glass pipe is recommended but may be difficult to find because they are often used for crack cocaine and risky to sell. Glass is good because the smoker can see into the bowl to monitor the melting and vaporization of the DMT or if it is leaking through the screen and running down the stem of the pipe.

The DMT is loaded into the pipe above a fine stainless steel mesh screen. The flame is kept about 1/2 inch away from the DMT. Enough should be drawn to heat and melt the DMT. The flame should never touch the DMT, which will destroy it. Placing a small amount of ash in the bottom of the pipe bowl holds the melted DMT before it vaporizes to prevent it from running down the pipe stem. A hash pipe works, but is less desirable because it is easy to burn the mouth with the hot vapor.

Smoking on a Carrier

More often, tryptamines are mixed with oregano, parsley leaves or marijuana and then smoked to produce effects similar to those from injections, except that they occur almost immediately and disappear more rapidly. Marijuana could be the best medium, because it is less harsh on the throat and lungs than parsley and because a lot of users like the combination. Some tryptamine enthusiasts object to mixtures with pot on the grounds that marijuana detracts from a tryptamine's clarity.

Parsley and other herbs can be converted into more neutral carriers by steeping them in water so as to extract most of their aromatic flavoring, and then drying the herb.

The smoke is very harsh and tastes a little like burning plastic. Many people like to have a bottle of water at hand to soothe their throats after the harsh DMT smoke. The breath is held as long as possible, then exhaled and a second toke is usually taken immediately. A buzzing or vibrational effect can come on fast but is not a reliable measure of the dosage. Experienced psychonauts advise that all of the premeasured DMT be consumed by taking large lungfuls and hold the breaths as long as possible.

Generally, it is advised that the pipe or joint not be passed from one person to the next, as is traditional with cannabis. Instead DMT is best taken in a predetermined dosage, which cannot be achieved when passing a pipe. The tripper has to draw in the full dosage in one breath because of the rapid habituation to DMT, which happens immediately after the first toke. Additional puffs have little effect until an hour or more has passed. For this reason, the last person to smoke usually packs the pipe for each user, each of whom smokes alone until his or her dosage is consumed. Effects usually come on before exhalation, usually in about 10 to 15 seconds. The rush is rapid and the person may experience a sense of vertigo, with the peak coming in 2 to 3 minutes.

Bigwood and Ott explain that when smoking DMT-soaked parsley, it can be difficult to gauge the proper dose. The only recourse, other than solvent extraction and isolation, is to use the "bioassay technique." Basically, this means trying a small amount of the mixture, then increasing the dose until the desired effects become apparent.

When smoked, fifteen to thirty milligrams of pure DMT is sufficient to produce hallucinogenic effects. This is a small amount, too small to be easily estimated without some reference. Bigwood and Ott suggest that the DMT be weighed out 15 to 30 milligrams as a reference. They recommend not measuring doses while inebriated.

Mescalito Ted cautions against smoking more than 25 mg. the first time. He points out that the does can be gradually increase over time with experience.

Jeremy Bigwood

As an oil, DMT is often mixed with an herb loose, bottled or in joints.

Safety

There are a number of safety concerns when using DMT. First off, DMT is metabolically destroyed by MAO. People who are on any form of medication need to take this into serious consideration—and should never use DMT if the medication is also a MAO-inhibitor because it makes DMT more potent. Additionally, there are a number of common foods and beverages that should not be taken with DMT.

Foods and Drinks Dangerous to Take with DMT

Sedatives & Tranquilizers	Yeast Extract
Antihistamines	Pineapple
Narcotics	Sauerkraut
Amphetamines	Pickled Herring
Asarone/Calamus	Soy Sauce
Aged cheese	Cream
Red wine	Avocado, overripe
Tryptophan	Bananas, overripe
Tyrosine	White Wine
Phenelalanine	Nutmeg
Alcohol	Oil of Dill
Ephedrine	Oil of Parsley
Macromerine	Liver
Anesthetics	Coffee
Beer	Figs, Raisins
Cocoa	Yogurt

These tryptamine compounds provoke intense experiences and should never be used in the care-free way marijuana often is. Smoking DMT while driving is foolhardy and extremely dangerous. Also, psychonauts with high blood pressure should definitely proceed only after consulting an experienced health practitioner because DMT is well known to increase blood pressure.

DMT trippers have poor motor control so a guide should be ready to take the pipe from the tripper's hand. The "free-fall" lasts for 4 to 8 minutes while the tripper looks asleep and will not want to be disturbed. Motor control is still shaky when coming out of the most intense part of the experience, so the tripper should remain seated for ten minutes or more. After about a half-hour the tripper will be "down" but still a little euphoric, and completely back to normal after about an hour.

Preparing the Setting

Set and setting are extremely influential during the DMT state, which is a magnifying, creative and sensitizing experience. Infinity Ayes, who began his DMT psychonaut explorations at Millbrook when Leary and Alpert (later to become Ram Dass) were there, notes that DMT is a weaver. Whatever you give DMT, it weaves this into patterns. Intention is everything, Ayes emphasizes.

Doing DMT is an adventure into the unknown, an experiment or series of explorations in which there is a great deal of trial and error. Psychological state is crucial. DMT should never be used if one is tense, anxious, worried, tired or over-wrought in any way.

The setting should be free from unexpected intrusions, like ringing telephones. Best is a room that is brightly lit but with indirect light. The colors tend to get too intense in full sunlight. When the setting is too dark, the visions tend to be muted. There should be a comfortable place to sit where the psychonaut can lie back to rest the head during the trance. DMT should definitely not be smoked while standing, because of the potential for falling and being injured.

Dosages

DET and DPT are more potent than DMT. The dosage for DMT is 40 mg., whereas the dose for 5-methoxy-DMT is 5 to 10 mg. Yet, even 15 to 20 mg. of DMT is sufficient to give strong effects when smoked. In most of the hospital studies, about 50 mg. of DMT was injected intramuscularly.

Experienced psychonauts recommend a dosage of 40-50 mg. The dosage should always be weighed out carefully and never simply eyeballed. Doses under 40 mg. tend to not display the full range of DMT effect. Below 25 mg. dosages yield physical and psychedelic effects but little more. Dosages over 55 mg. can be very "heavy" and could be recommended for seasoned DMT experimenters only.

A lightweight trip can be achieved by mixing 25 mg. of DMT with cannabis and smoked to achieve a pleasant giggly mood with an occasional breaking through of abstract hallucinatory patterns.

Effects

The experience is characterized by a "rush" similar to that from amyl nitrate. Visuals, intense thoughts and. perhaps, bodily sensations last for five to ten minutes. In *Psychedelic Chemistry,* Michael Valentine Smith compared 5-methoxy-DMT's effects to having an elephant sit on your head.

The DMT peak lasts for three to ten minutes, and is over in twenty to thirty minutes. DET and DPT, which have more subtle effects than DMT, may take a few minutes to register, although, as Alan Birnbaum writes in regard to DPT, "some people have reported to be immediately immersed in the light on the first toke." DET lasts about an hour when smoked. The most intense part of a DPT experience is over in about twenty minutes.

After taking a toke, first-time users often say they don't feel anything and then suddenly become silent in mid-sentence. The observable physical changes include pupil dilation, increased pulse rate and blood pressure, and, in some instances, dizziness, nausea or tremor. Stephen Szara and his associates examined such effects closely in a series of papers, concluding that these were minor problems. Nonetheless, psychonauts with high blood pressure should consult an appropriate health care professional before using DMT and related compounds.

Mind-Blowing

The suddenness and intensity with which DMT
comes on can be somewhat alarming, so much so
that, as Grinspoon and Bakalar remarked, the term
"mind-blowing" might have been invented for this
drug. The DMT experience has been described as
"melting into" or "fusing" with the floor, like your
heart is stopping, or that your "life-force" is somehow ebbing away. When the experience is over, the
user feels normal again but may worry, more than
with other psychedelics, about such physical feelings, particularly if the compound was inadvisably
used while alone.

According to Michael Valentine Smith, DMT and
related compounds taste and smell like burning
plastic when smoked and are harder to smoke than
hash. He says that there is, however, no evidence
for the notion that they are damaging.

If an insufficient amount has entered the brain,
it is unlikely that a user will get that strong a DMT
effects. Twenty minutes must elapse before a
second try. But even if a higher level of experience
is not attained, the effects can still be impressive,
approximating a very colorful, intense hash high,
and can be extended if there is an adequate supply
on hand. Residual DET and DPT effects can also be
sustained by taking continual pipefuls.

Synergy

Sai-Halasz, who worked with Szara, reported that
DMT was potentiated by pretreatment with serotonin antagonists like methysergide. He demonstrated
such potentiation could be diminished by pretreatment with monoamine oxidase inhibitors.

Generally DMT is inactive when taken orally. A gram of DMT, well over thirty times the dose needed to achieve effects from smoking, has been swallowed without perceptible psychoactivity. When these substances pass into the stomach, they are attacked by the enzyme monoamine oxidase, which hacks the molecule apart. However, in the company of MAO-inhibitors, like the β-carbolines associated with *yage*, these tryptamines become resistant to quick metabolism and thus remain effective when taken orally.

Synergy of DMT & LSD

One inhalation of the concentrated smoke, and the world melts into its patterning constituents. A second inhalation, and the body becomes transfixed with a silence so deep and so startling that within it a tear would fall as a torrent. A third inhalation, and sentience visibly radiates itself from everywhere: plants and animals are transfigured to their sacred essence and pebbles sparkle like self-conscious, magical jewels. But the balance is delicate. The vision can detonate along with the nervous system that falters before it. Such experiences, though often quite horrible, are no more than a widow's mite in the table stakes of consciousness, for under the guidance of the LSDMT synergy, vast realms of perfect attunement may also occur, and the stellar brilliance of the clear-light void shines from everywhere, from everything, inside and out.

—Walter Anirman
Sky Cloud Mountain

Legality

DPT and 5-methoxy-DMT are still legal and have been used in certain circles for years. Alan Birnbaum, from the Native American Church of New York, wrote to the DEA about the legal status of several DMT-like compounds.

The federal government has tried to exert more control over this type of psychoactive. For example, in the *Federal Registry*, the Deputy Administrator of the Drug Enforcement Administration (DEA) on April 4th, 2003 issued the final rule to temporarily place alpha-methyltryptamine (AMT) and 5-methoxy-N, N-diisopropyltryptamine (5-MeO-DIPT) into Schedule 1 of the Controlled Substances Act "to avoid an imminent hazard to the public safety."

4

Mental Effects

of DMT

MT has been the most studied and used of the short-acting tryptamines. Almost everyone who's had a good lungful has been astonished by the rapidity and vividness of the high. With eyes open, there appears a "retinal circus," where perception of the external world is overlaid with moving, fascinating, brightly colored patterns.

With the eyes closed, trippers become aware of swirling patterns, often geometric in shape. Many people become ecstatic or euphoric, others become meditative and concentrate on the hallucinations with eyes closed. Sometimes there can develop a feeling of foreboding or paranoia during the initial stages of the inebriation. Generally, the effects are enjoyable and most trippers are astonished by how rapidly DMT can produce such profound effects, which have such short duration.

Ayes has argued that DMT, according to one's readiness, will manifest on one of three levels: 1) the design and symbol level; 2) the messenger level; and 3) an ineffable level of total communication with The Mystery. He likens these levels to a kind of consciousness staircase where as, one climbs the stairs, one achieves higher levels of astonishment.

At the end of the flash of visions most people have an after-vision of circular interlocking patterns of intense colors, which has been known as the DMT Dome. By 10 to 12 minutes, the visions will have subsided, but patterns may still be seen with closed eyes.

At this point many people experience a flood of information rushing through their minds. Some have a tape recorder running and they begin talking as soon as they come out of the visionary state—not trying for complete sentences, just getting the ideas out.

Sometimes when users are getting really high on DMT and "breakthrough", they worry that they may not find their way back to their body. Experienced psychonauts advise trusting in body and psyche.

After his first use of DMT, Humphry Osmond remained silent for some time and then responded with: "My ... word!" Another person who had received some DMT through the mail from a friend, assumed it was a new kind of cannabis. After smoking what she thought was a joint, she telegraphed her friend: "What—repeat—What was that?!"

Alan Watts said the DMT experience was like "being fired out of the muzzle of an atomic cannon." He later reevaluated DMT, calling it "amusing but relatively uninteresting" compared to LSD, mescaline, psilocybin and cannabis.

An example of how DMT's effects may be meaningful, evoking more than a sequence of kaleidoscopic images, comes from Ram Dass, who was debating with Leary whether the word ecstasy should be used in describing LSD and psilocybin trips. Ram Dass thought it would "just get everybody thinking about orgies", whereas Leary said he liked the word's derivation from ex—or ek—stasis—going out of the static.

Ram Dass had received a huge, hand-embroidered robe brought by a lama from Tibet. Though appreciative, he didn't know what to do with the robe and decided to wear it while using DMT to consider this question about ecstasy. The smell of incense from the robe surrounded him as he shot DMT into his thigh and lay down.

Ram Dass Experiences Ecstasy

I found myself walking down some very wide steps into what seemed like a Roman or Greek scene. Torches lit the stairway of a stone castle. I walked down into an underground grotto, where I looked through a door into a room. Inside was a kidney-shaped indoor swimming pool, and beyond that were groves of trees. Nymph-like figures were diving into the pool, which was surrounded by silver statues. I got the feeling of intense sensuality, of a Dionysian, orgy-like place.

I stood at the door, sure I wasn't going to go into this "Sin City"—not me, afraid of my impulses. But then I noticed that one of the statues was of Timothy, who was laughing. I said, "See, I knew I was right!"

Then, suddenly, I was whisked away in an elevator. It felt like being shot up in the Trade Center Building in New York City.

Then, just as suddenly, it stopped. I found myself in a dome that was luminously white. The light wasn't inside or out—the whole thing was luminous. A more intense light emanated from the center skylight. There were many people in the room, gathered mainly in the center and looking upward.

I crowded in to see what they were looking at. Finally, I reached the center and could look up. I discovered I was looking up into absolutely clear light. I'm looking directly at the light, and it's totally purifying me.

At the most ecstatic moment in this experience, I heard a laugh. I turned to look, and, at the edge of the crowd, there stood Timothy. I realized that he was telling me that this was "ecstasy", too.

I took off the robe, went down to see Timothy, and said, "'Ecstasy' is a great word. Let's use it."

—Ram Dass

Set and Setting

Bigwood and Ott advise that it is best to be in a calm and relaxed state. They say that it is unwise to smoke DMT when tense or anxious. Set and setting have a big impact. Some people have frightening, even terrifying experiences on DMT. Because the transition into the altered state is so rapid and so intense, some people have concluded when they saw religious archetypes arise that they had been lured into a pact with the Devil. Some people have worried that they might "never come back."

Possibly the best published example of the negative side of the DMT experience is found in Jean Houston's *The Varieties of Psychedelic Experience*, where she presents an illustration of bad set and setting and the fearful results that can manifest under such conditions. Houston had been up for three days and two nights working on a manuscript when she experimented with DMT. She described the place as "a dirty, dingy, insanely cluttered pesthole." She said that she was told she "would see God". Instead she experienced what she described as "the most terrifying three minutes" of her life—seemed an eternity. After injecting DMT Houston made "a final effort at ultimate visions," and a face of God appeared. It was a very wise monkey. Houston burst out laughing.

Terence McKenna was an outspoken proponent of DMT. What he had to say on this subject may seem outrageous—as though, as an Irishman, he had kissed the Blarney Stone. Perhaps more than anyone else, McKenna captured the essence of the experience. "Language cannot describe it—accurately," McKenna began. "Therefore I will inaccurately describe it. The rest is now lies."

Elves in the Dome

You are propelled into this "place." First of all—and why, I don't know—you have the impression that you are underground. Far underground. You can't say why, but there's just this feeling of immense weight above you. But you're in a large space, a vaulted dome. People even call it "The DMT Dome." I have had people say to me, "Have you been under the dome?" And I knew exactly what they meant.

So you burst into this space. It's lit, sock-eted lighting, some kind of indirect lighting you can't quite locate. But what is astonish-ing and immediately riveting is that in this place there are entities—there are these things which I call "self-transforming ma-chine elves."

It's like a Bugs Bunny cartoon gone mad. And all of this energy—they are elves. This is what elves are. It's this weird thing where they love you—or they like you a lot—but you can tell that their sense of humor is weird.

There is this "You must be on your toes" thing. Don't let these guys get behind you. They are tricky. And their elfin humor may not be your idea of a good time.

It's a feeling of being with people that I can't trust, but who want to help me, and who seem to be trying to cut a deal. Well, then they say "Do!"

And the objects that they make have the peculiar ability to themselves generate this "linguistic stuff" which condenses as other objects. So beings are making objects, showing you objects, the objects are turning into beings and making other objects, these beings and objects. They jump into your body and disappear into your body, and then they jump back out, waving these things, just throwing this stuff in all directions.

The word that comes to mind is: they are Zany. And then I remembered. "I know where I felt like this"—I felt like this in the Crawford Market in Bombay when I had a kilo of Gold in my pocket and I was trying to trade it for hashish, and I was surrounded by all these Arab hash traders, and they were saying, "We're your friend. Just wait. Don't worry...."

—Terance McKenna

Idiosyncratic Nature

No two "dimethyl trips" are alike. Anyone who has smoked enough DMT to be launched beyond the initial threshold stage will almost always describe the experience they've had in superlatives. Such as total free-fall, visitation to another kind of mental universe, like something from a flying saucer, plant wisdom provoking "pre-genetic encodation," the most idiosyncratic thing there is, a fantastic visionary activator, as intense as any drug ever should get, the closest thing to the Holy Grail that I've ever come in contact with, pipelines into a kind of planetary mind, an access code into "hyper-dimensional reality" and "It gave me goose-bumps."

When asked if one would be taking a risk when using DMT, McKenna answered, "Yes. It's tremendously dangerous. The danger is the possibility of death by astonishment. And you must prepare yourself for this eventuality, because you are so amazed. I mean astounded. When was the last time you were genuinely astounded? I mean I think you can go your whole damned life without being astounded! And this is astonishment, you know, raised to the nth degree—to the point that your jaw hangs . . ."

The Carrot

I ingested DMT and almost immediately found myself in an Escher kind of setting. I was amazed that I was able to walk about this tableau—even walk through the doors. I enjoyed tramping along Escher's fantastic staircases, examining the Moorish facades, so gleamingly green and full of motion!

Then, suddenly, I was outside on a flat, dusty landscape. The sunlight felt great on my browned back, even though quite hot, as I watched with fascination the shimmering heat waves. A pickup arrived, filled with workers atop a load of bagged—carrots? To my surprise, a half-dozen people jumped out of the truck and hauled the large bags, weighing perhaps twenty-five or thirty pounds, into a warehouse next to us. They lined the inside perimeter with carrot sacks to a height of about six feet.

When the staking was complete, I quite rapidly "came down." I became aware of the setting I was in and the people who were with me. I spoke to the others about how remarkably convincing the carrot scenario had been. I was particularly struck by the "editing" and use of unusual camera angles in the "film" I had seen of the carrot-sack-unloading activity. It actually took me five or six minutes to realize that what had transpired was not that I had tuned in to some documentary—perhaps, I thought, from the U.S. Agriculture Dept.

I was quite unaware for awhile that the carrot-unloading enactment was actually a product of my own mind—mistakenly presuming, it seems, that I had witnessed a work by cinematic professionals. Only gradually did it dawn on me that what I had envisioned had been produced and directed by my mind alone! I know not how or why this particular "Carrot Movie" could or should have arisen. It just struck me that I had been witnessing an odd kind of "training film." The presentation had been so clear, convincing and edgy that I believed, for just awhile, that I had picked up on some documentary that elsewhere existed.

I wondered if "my totem" is a carrot! Was I being led along by some kind of carrot? Beats me!

—Peter Stafford

Reed Canary Grass

As for the potency of Reed Canary Grass, James DeKorne, author of *Psychedelic Shamanism*, has commented that he had two crushed capsules of *Phalaris* concentrate which he wanted to salvage as an *ayahuasca* admixture. So he placed the material in a shot glass full of alcohol to redissolve this extract. DeKorne forget about it for about two weeks, during which time the alcohol evaporated, leaving behind a gummy tar. He was about to throw it out, but then on a sudden whim wondered what would happen if he smoked the stuff. So DeKorne redissolved the tar and evaporated it onto some oregano as an inert smoking medium. He recounted his experience: "Imagine my surprise when, in a very casual set and setting (the bedroom, early afternoon), I took one inhalation of this essence and found my mind immediately blasted into a cerebral hurricane of rapidly pulsing white light. Fortunately, I already knew what a DMT flash is like, so I was not totally taken by surprise."

You may wonder if these weird, often cartoony experiences regularly prompted by DMT ever have any long-lasting effects. Often the after-effects can last a lifetime as is the case with Stephen Gaskin, founder of The Farm commune in Tennessee, and author of Cannabis Spirituality and Monday Night Class.

When I Fall in Love It Will Be on DMT

I fell in love with my wife Ina May on DMT. We sat down. Ina May on the couch and me on the floor at her feet, and we lit off a pipe each. I looked in Ina May's eyes, and every edge, every line, every detail became electric and alive with threads of color running through it, until the entire environment was neon, psychedelically, pulsingly, crawlingly alive, and lit. She looked into my eyes and smiled as we lit up the environment, and played with our DMT.

As I looked at her," Gaskin continued, "I fell telepathically into her and saw that we matched up to many decimal places and were really as telepathic as we could be. It just blew me away. She was with someone else at the time. I looked at her for a second, and I had to put my eyes down, because I couldn't keep looking at her, or I knew I would get so far in that I'd never get back out. It was too late.

This kind of thing happens to people. Get stoned with somebody, look a them, fall in love with them, and the whole rest of the material plane doesn't matter. And then, suddenly, as fast as it came on, coming down a perpendicular square-edge drop-off, everything will be perfectly ordinary again. After it was gone and I hit bottom, it took me a second or two to forgive myself for ever coming down from it. As it turned out over the last thirty years, in many ways, we never did come down from it.

—Stephen Gaskin

DET Effects

DET doesn't have the visual impact of DMT but when smoked it does evoke intense, pleasurable states of mind, which last for about an hour. Meditators have noticed that they can lock themselves into a lotus position much more easily than before. The DET experience can be built upon by repeated inhalations, with some users reporting that they have begun to "vibrate" and "raise Kundalini energy." Some users find that their eyes turn backward, as in a state of religious ecstasy.

Among those who have experienced DET with religious intensity is Alan Birnbaum. "DET is the first psychedelic which convinced me that the psychedelic is a Primeval Light Being which is God, the Creator. We had smoked it in a large hookah and it was so clear and so bright—unmistakable—it was a Being."

The most extensive report on the effects of DET was prepared by Boszormenyi, Der and Nagy in the *Journal of Mental Sciences*. They described trials in thirty normal and forty-one psychiatric subjects who were given 0.7 to 0.8 mg./kg. intramuscularly. They concluded that DET was more satisfactory than LSD or mescaline in increasing communication and aiding therapy because of its shorter duration of action. They said that DET was among the best and least noxious psychotogenic agents.

After the session some of Boszormenyi's subjects showed an interest in art and writing. Two took up painting. Several subjects, who were professional authors, compared their experiences with spontaneous inspiration. One young poet reported that he felt an enormous drive to write, to put down the marvelous feelings. Boszormenyi suggested that the increase in creativity resulted from "the emergence of ancient desires and drives which forced the person to satisfy them by creating."

When smoked DET is like grass, but you get very high and are still functional. There is a little hallucination, and a little color distortion. It's not as intense as DMT, and you can do things behind it— like go to lectures or run around the streets. With DMT and acid you're often astonished, wondering what's happening, whereas with DET you know you're on it.

DPT Effects

DPT is not very widely used, but those who have tried it agree that it produces psychedelic or "peak" experiences. Much of its application in psychotherapy has taken place in Europe, under the supervision of such specialists as Dr. Hanscarl Leuner, who published a book in German on psycholytic therapy. Initial reports in the U.S. came from the Maryland Psychiatric Research Center, which used this drug in conjunction with therapy at Spring Grove Hospital near Baltimore.

In the *Journal of Psychedelic Drugs,* doctors on the Spring Grove team discussed their findings about "The Peak Experience Variable in DPT-Assisted Psychotherapy with Cancer Patients." They state that it evokes peak experiences "with sufficient potency and reliability to permit us to study their impact on human behavior."

The research team administered DPT to cancer patients who were expected to live at least three months and who were suffering major psychological stress. The goal was to evoke what William James called the "noetic" quality of peak experiences, about which he said, "Although so similar to states of feeling, [these] mystical states seem to those who experience them to be also states of knowledge. They are states of insight into depths of truth unplumbed by the discursive intellect."

Results indicated some clinical improvement. Patients receiving the DPT (peakers) showed improvement in "capacity for intimate contact," suggesting the enhancement of a quality of interpersonal openness that might mitigate the isolation and lack of meaningful communication often experienced by terminally ill patients and their closest family members.

Nonetheless, this team concluded from its experiments with DPT that peak experiences may constitute an intrinsic element of effective psychotherapy for some persons and that rapid therapeutic progress in the course of short-term psychotherapy with cancer patients is indicated by this study. In a comment also pertinent for anyone considering use of DPT, they observed that when a peak experience does occur, its continuing relevance for daily living may be strongly dependent on the degree to which the associated insights are assimilated or transferred into the everyday self-concept and world view of the patient.

The Spring Grove team subsequently administered DPT as "assisted psychotherapy" to alcoholics. A year after the experience the group given DPT "showed an advantage in positive outcome measures", particularly in regard to Occupational Adjustment and Sobriety when compared to the two control groups. Those given DPT may have temporarily experienced a substantial number of peak reactions, the authors wrote, and may have temporarily experienced a more positive mode of functioning. Later follow-ups, however, revealed few long-term differences among the three groups, a result that "would seem to indicate that the DPT group did not know how to integrate their new modes of functioning into the everyday patterns of their lives."

5

Tryptamine Constituents

n both *Anadenanthera* and *Virola* snuffs, the active principles are indolic alkaloids, either "open-chained" or "closed-ring" tryptamines. The "open-chained" group includes DMT and 5-methoxy-DMT, as well as bufotenine (which appears to be non-psychoactive). DMT predominates in the species *Virola calophylla*, but in other species the greatest psychic contribution comes from the very short-acting 5-methoxy-DMT.

Trace amounts of the "open-chained" DMT-N-oxide and 5-hydroxy-DMT-N-oxide, as well as "closed-ring" tryptamines 2-methyl- and 1,2-dimethyl-7-methoxytetrahydro-β-carboline, are present in both *Anadenanthera* and *Virola* snuffs, adding somewhat to their effects. *Virolas* also contain small quantities of 6-methoxy-DMT and monoethyltryptamine.

Side-Chains

Brimblecombe and Pinder discuss the chemistry of this compound-cluster and its effects in *Hallucinogenic Agents*. Many of these compounds display little psychoactivity. Of interest to our discussion here are the diallyl, dibutyl and diisopropyl analogs, the last having about twelve times the potency of DMT.

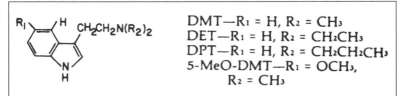

DMT—R_1 = H, R_2 = CH_3
DET—R_1 = H, R_2 = CH_2CH_3
DPT—R_1 = H, R_2 = $CH_2CH_2CH_3$
5-MeO-DMT—R_1 = OCH_3,
R_2 = CH_3

Cemical Family Portrait of Major Short-Acting Tryptamines

Cerebrospinal Tryptamines

L-tryptophan is an essential amino acid prevalent throughout the animal world. It is the only one that is an indole and is generally considered the basic building block for the indolealkalylamines, which include most of the compounds discussed as entheogens or psychedelics. Neither *l* tryptophan nor bufotenine are considered psychoactive—although bufotenine was once thought to be at higher dosages. However, both are cross-tolerant with LSD, as is DMT, which suggests that their molecules may occupy the same or related receptor-sites in the brain. By contrast, DMT is not cross-tolerant with psilocybin or mescaline.

Much attention has gone into seeking a "psychotogen," a chemical manufactured in an abnormal brain and nervous system that causes psychosis. Most psychedelic drugs cannot possibly play this role, because, as Grinspoon and Bakalar explain, tolerance develops too quickly for a persistent effect. They say that the main exception is DMT, which has been identified as an endogenous compound in the brains of rats and human beings. The enzyme responsible for its synthesis and the sites where it is absorbed by nerve terminals have also been discovered. Grinspoon and Bakalar note that LSD and 5-methoxy-DMT seem to displace DMT at those sites, which may also be serotonin receptors.

In the late 1970s Dr. Samuel Christian and his associates at the University of Alabama in Birmingham's Neurosciences Program identified DMT, 5-methoxy-DMT, N-methyltryptamine and tryptamine in human cerebrospinal fluid and brain. Dr. Wolfgang Vogel of the Jefferson Medical College in Philadelphia isolated 5-methoxy-DMT in brain tissue.

If DMT and 5-methoxy-DMT are neurotransmitters, as many researchers think, then an excess of them may be a cause of schizophrenia. Observing dramatic increases of DMT in the spinal fluid of animals and humans during extreme stress, Dr. Christian hypothesized that the tendency among some people to develop mental aberrations might reflect "a genetic predisposition to excessive DMT production as a response to stress." Later work, reported by L. Corbett, Christian and others in the *British Journal of Psychiatry* indicated that schizophrenics do not have higher levels of DMT in their brains than control subjects. Research in this intriguing area continues.

Synthesizing DMT

Methods of synthesizing DMT were published in
*The Turn-On Book, T he Psych edelic Guide to P repa-
ration of the Eucharist* and several short pamphlets.
Analogs that are still legal can be synthesized by
substituting equal molar amounts of source materials other than dimethylamine, which yields DMT, or
diethylamine, which yields DET. Using
dipropylamine as a starter yields DPT,
methylethylamine yields methylethyltryptamine,
methylpropylamine yields methylpropyltryptamine,
ethylpropylamine yields ethylpropyltryptamine, etc.

Processes for synthesizing short-acting
tryptamines are fairly simple and don't require
much in the way of equipment, but they involve a
risk of explosion. Also, purchases of several of the
source materials are watched by the Federal Drug
Enforcement Agency. One of these is lithium aluminum hydride ($LiAlH_4$), which is dangerous if it
comes in contact with water molecules—as is
usually required at the end of these processes. A
chemist describes an experiment:

A Chemist's Experiment

I placed a gray chunk of it in a stainless
steel pot and left it exposed to the air to see
what would happen. When nothing appre-
ciable occurred, I got a hammer and banged
it—which ignited it.

It then burned white hot right through the
stainless steel pot and continued to burn on
the floor. Of course, one cannot use water
to put it out because it reacts with water

causing not only a more vigorous reaction but also releasing hydrogen which, as you know, will explode violently itself when it reaches a certain concentration of O_2. Luckily for him, it was a small piece.

—Anonymous Chemist

Extraction

As for *Phalaris arundinacea* and *P. aquatica,* Jim DeKorne in *Psychedelic Shamanism* gives instructions for easy extraction.

1) Pulverize the grass cuttings as much as you can.

2) Add water to make a pourable soup.

3) Add an acid—such as white vinegar, lemon juice or acetic acid—just enough to bring the pH down to about 5. Simmer in a closed cooker overnight.

4) Strain the plant matter through cheese-cloth, then through a paper coffee filter. Discard the bulk roughage.

5) Add a small amount of a defatting solvent, such as methylene chloride, ether, chloroform or naphtha (Coleman fuel or lighter fluid) to remove the oils and fats in the solution. Shake the mixture and put it aside long enough to separate into two layers, the bottom one aqueous, the other solvent.

6) Discard the solvent, along with unwanted oils and fats, via a separatory funnel or a turkey baster.

7) Dissolve ammonium hydroxide or regular lye crystals (the drain cleaner called sodium hydroxide) in water, and then add this in small increments to the aqueous solution, shaking each time and testing it until eventually the pH reaches 9 or 10. This transforms the alkaloids into their freebase form, so they are accessible to extraction.

8) Add a solvent, such as Coleman starting fuel, that amounts to about 10% of the aqueous solution—keeping the container closed tightly so the solvent won't evaporate from the solution.

9) Shake this solution twice a day, and then remove the solvent layer—which has a darker tint, usually yellowish or reddish-brown—after 24 hours, and then one week, two weeks and three weeks later adding each time some fresh solvent to the aqueous solution until this extraction is complete.

10) Pour the combined solvent fractions into a shallow baking dish or pan and allow this to evaporate in an open space free of flames or sparks. "The residue remaining after the evaporation contains the alkaloids, and may be put into gelatin capsules. If it is unduly gummy, one may add small amounts of ordinary flour to the gum until it thickens.

Legal Status

State and federal laws enacted from 1966 to 1969 made DMT illegal. Both DMT and DET were included in Schedule I of the Controlled Substances Act of 1970. Source materials for these compounds were put on a watch status as well. Soon supplies dried up, and both DMT and DET became rare items—a situation that has persisted since the 1970s.

DMT was also identified as a normal constituent of human blood—though its function is as yet obscure, prompting Bigwood and Ott to comment: "Public Law 91-513 specifically proscribes unauthorized possession of any material which contains DMT in any quantity. Under this law ... any individual human being is guilty of such possession."

6

Ayahuasca

 udging from the richness of associated mythology, the use of *ayahuasca,* pronounced EYE-a-was-ca. for visionary experiences appears to be primeval. Pre-Columbian rock drawings are similar to contemporary *ayahuasqueros* paintings, which are said to represent *yage* visions. However, the earliest known record of the practices associated with this botanical wasn't set down until the middle of the 19th Century.

Harmaline and other harmala alkaloids appear throughout the plant world and are the principle psychoactive ingredient in the "magical" beverage *yage*, pronounced yah-hey. These substances are also present in cigarettes and even in the human pineal gland.

Although these three-ringed compounds are widespread in the plant kingdom, their use as a entheogen is known in only two specific, geographically separate traditions. First is the scraping of the bark of *Banisteriopsis* vines to make a drink in the Amazon, and second, ingestion of the seeds of Syrian

Jeremy Bigwood

Banisteriopsis caapi, *the Amazonian "vine of the soul."*

rue—*Peganum harmala*, a wild desert shrub, in the Near East. The Amazonian practices are better documented and colorfully illustrate the purgative, healing, visual, telepathic, sexual, artistic, religious and therapeutic potentials in entheogens.

Yage, a psychedelic drink used by natives and urban dwellers in northwestern South America, is made from the outer bark of this vine. Psychedelic constituents are harmaline, harmine and d-1,2,3,4-tetrahydro-harmine.

The first widely read description of *yage* practices was published in 1858 by Manuel Villavicencio, an Ecuadorian geographer. The experience made him feel he was "flying" to most marvelous places. Richard Spruce, a British schoolteacher, was among the early explorers to make the perilous journey into the Amazon. Spruce almost died of dysentery and malaria but survived to become one of botany's greatest collectors. In the early 1850s, while exploring the upper Rio Negro of the Brazilian Amazon, he described *yage* and its sources, its preparation and its effects upon himself in *Notes of a Botanist on the Amazon and Andes.* Unfortunately, Spruce's experience was mainly getting sick.

Richard Spruce was the first to write about *yage* ingestion and his name is attached to the *Banisteriopsis caapi* species, the most important botanical source of harmala alkaloids.

Spruce suspected that additives were responsible for the psychoactivity of the beverage, although he noted that *Banisteriopsis* by itself was considered mentally activating. The samples he sent to England for chemical analysis were misplaced and not assayed until more than a century later, when they were examined in 1966 when they were found to be still psychoactive.

Describing how natives responded, Spruce reported that users of the drink were able "to foresee and answer accurately in difficult cases, be it to reply opportunely to ambassadors from other tribes in a question of war; to decipher plans of the enemy through the medium of this magic drink and take proper steps for attack and defense; to ascertain, when a relative is sick, what sorcerer has put on the hex; to carry out a friendly visit to other tribes; to welcome foreign travelers or, at least to make sure of the love of their womenfolk."

Several early explorers of northwestern South America—Martius, Crevaux, Orton, Koch-Grunberg and others—referred to *ayahuasca, yage* and *caapi*, citing a forest liana but offering little detail. In the early 20th Century, it was learned that the use of *Banisteriopsis* vines for healing, initiatory and shamanic rites extended to Peru and Bolivia.

Richard Spruce

Sparked Interest

Because of the considerable interest in the psychedelic experience that the introduction of LSD trig-
gered reports about *yage* that ordinarily would
have been restricted to the technical literature
received fairly wide circulation. *Psychedelic Review*
and *The Psychedelic Reader,* for instance, reprinted
Richard Evans Schultes' discussions about *yage,*
which spread the word about the vine and its use
for divinatory and prophetic purposes.

Many researchers traveled to South America in
search of *ayahuasqueros,* hoping to have a personal
yage experience. The brothers Dennis and Terence
McKenna recounted an *ayahuasca-psilocybe* experience that lasted allegedly for a month in the jungle.
Their fascinating speculative volume, *The Invisible
Landscape,* called attention to *yage* while considering topics of mind-body interactions.

Bruce Lamb's *Wizard of the Upper Amazon*
presents the romantic turn-of-the-century jungle
story of Manuel Cordova-Rios, who became an
ayahuasquero after being kidnapped at age fifteen
by the Ayahuaca Indians of
Peru. This account details his
use of *Banisteriopsis* in
hunting, healing and telepa-
thy—including group visions.

The Story of Manuel Córdova-Rios
**WIZARD OF THE
UPPER AMAZON**
by F. BRUCE LAMB

Interest in harmala com-
pounds arose as well from
reports that among the
Jivaro headhunting tribes of
the upper Amazon—and the
Cashinahua of Peru—the

A romantic tale.

"dream" contents of *yage* experiences were commonly regarded as constituting more important guiding principles than ordinary consciousness.

Andrew Weil said that no drug plant has excited more interest than *yage*. In *The Marriage of the Sun and Moon,* he remembers during the 1960s Haight-Ashbury being offered this "tiger drug", so called because it was said to inspire visions of big jungle cats. Later, he tried to find a more authentic experience in Colombia.

Perhaps the best wide-ranging examination of the various states of *ayahuasca* experience comes from a professor of psychology at the Hebrew University in Jerusalem, Bernard Shamon, in *The Antipodes of the Mind.* He tried the experience himself many times and interviewed natives, city folk, shamans and travellers. Shamon lays out what he thinks is a structure that can be applied to the experience, and which he also feels is applicable to other entheogenic usage.

In a review of Shamon's book, William Benson drew attention in a lengthy *Human Nature Review* article to the simultaneous but distinct consciousnesses that often are evoked in *yage* experiencing, which he likens to "two or three interacting contrapuntal voices in a Bach fugue."

Psychedelic Tourism

Several groups offer journeys to the Amazon with the idea of pilgrims taking *ayahuasca* under their auspices. Ayahuasca SpiritQuest, for example, advertises "Transformative workshop retreats exploring the essence of traditional shamanic Ayahuasca healing practices and ethnobotany in the heart of the Peruvian Amazon."

In another instance, Ayahuasca-Wasi considers itself a "Transpersonal Shamanism Research Project," and offers a "seven-day Experimental Seminar in the heart of the Peruvian Rainforest." It promises a stimulating, responsible and safe experience "for those who are looking for an authentic way to pursue their personal quest". The group claims that the sessions are a step in the initiation into shamanism and declare that "true shamanic consciousness can be acquired by following the principles demonstrated in the seminar for many years."

Jonathan Ott called attention to the hordes of curious from the USA and Europe visiting the rainforest to partake in this "jungle drug", usually paying high prices for the privilege of "Ayahuasca Tourism." Ott says that as a result some people have put considerable effort into creation of temperate-zone analogs of *ayahuasca*, which will yield an entheogenic potion similar to the tropical *ayahuasca*." Dennis McKenna, brother of Terence and a professor of chemistry, proposed the name *Ayahuasca borealis* for these particular analogs.

Patenting Attempt

Believe it or not, the U.S. Patent Office granted a patent for use of *ayahuasca* to someone from the U.S. in the late 1990s. However, in response to a request for reexamination by the Coordinating Body for the Indigenous Organizations of the Amazon Basin, the Coalition for Amazonian Peoples and Their Environment, and lawyers at the Center for International Environmental Law, the U.S. Patent and Trademark Office in November 1999 rejected the claim to private rights over this plant.

The basis for rejection was that publications describing *Banisteriopsis caapi* were known and available before the filing of the patent application. Patent law prevents the proprietary assumption of use of such a plant if described in printed publications more than one year prior to the date of a patent application.

Given that *ayahuasca* has been used in sacred indigenous ceremonies throughout the Amazon by well over 70 separate tribes for some two millennia, David Rothshchild, director of the Amazon Coalition, quite correctly declared: "This patent never should have been issued in the first place."

7

Ayahuasca Use
& Effects

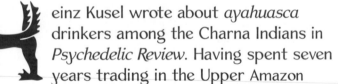

einz Kusel wrote about *ayahuasca* drinkers among the Charna Indians in *Psychedelic Review*. Having spent seven years trading in the Upper Amazon region, he observed that "Indians and low-class mestizos alike visit the *ayahuasquero* when they are ailing, or think they need a general checkup, or want to make an important decision, or simply because they feel like it."

Marlene Dobkin de Rios studied *yage's* uses in folk healing in an urban setting in Peru, which she reported upon in *The Visionary Vine*. A professor of anthropology at California State College at Fullerton, de Rios observed that the supply of *ayahuasca* was becoming depleted in the jungles near Iquitos, site of her investigations, and that suppliers had to search much further for it.

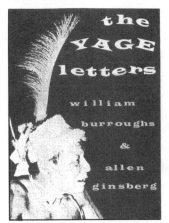

the YAGE letters

william
burroughs
&
allen
ginsberg

Search for the magic drink.

Although her fieldwork was done largely in a slum section of Iquitos, de Rios saw *ayahuasca* being used throughout the region for religious and magic rituals to receive a protective spirit or divine guidance from the plant spirit; for diagnosing and treating disease; for divination to learn an enemy's plans, for instance, or to check on a spouse's fidelity; for witchcraft to prevent harm caused by others' malice or to cause harm to others; and for pleasure.

Yage has been absolutely taboo on occasion for women. When a trumpet signalled the start of the puberty rites for the Yurupari boys, female members of the tribe fled into the jungle to avoid a death penalty for their seeing the ceremony or even the drink. In other regions, it was thought that if a woman set eyes on prepared *caapi,* the vine would be rendered ineffective. More generally, women were allowed to drink *yage* but were discouraged if they wished to become adepts, which frequently involved a year of regularly drinking *ayahuasca* infusions spiked with tobacco juice.

Rituals

There are several types of ritual. In the "official works" of a religion based on *yage* use, the community will dance for up to 12 hours in a specific formation and rhythm to generate an energy current, with the Daime—a tea made from the vine *Banistereopsis caapi* and, generally, also the leaves

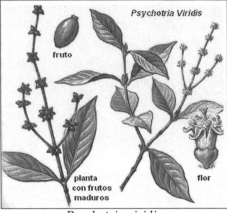

Psychotria viridis

of the plant *Psychotria viridis*—being drunk several times during the night. In the healing rituals, the participants generally sit around the altar and one or more people are the recipients of the healing. The deeper cause of the illness is often revealed during this procedure, in a vision.

A group called Friends of the Amazon Forest also recommends that to enhance the experience sexual orgasms three days before and three days after the ritual should be avoided. Practicing Tantra is highly recommended, however.

In fact, the Brazilian Federal Drug Council concluded that the Daime "religion" was a very positive influence in the community, encouraging social harmony and personal integration.

There are also moves towards organizing the healing works of the Daime, creating a center which will include not only the traditional healing rituals, but also psychotherapy, a clinic, a hospital and birthing center, along with training programs and workshops.

Medicine men's plants and rituals.

Richard Evans Schultes.

Effects

Schultes reported that the effects upon natives of the upper Rio Negro of Brazil, "with whom I have taken *caapi* many times, is pleasant, characterized amongst other strange effects by colored visual hallucinations. In excessive doses, it is said to bring on frighteningly nightmarish visions and a feeling of extremely reckless abandon, but consciousness is not lost nor is use of the limbs unduly affected."

Harmala Alone

The harmala experience by itself is mild. Some people have obtained psychedelic effects from Syrian Rue by consuming small amounts over the course of a day to circumvent nausea. Turner reported that concentrated harmala can be smoked for a more mindless body high, often accompanied by feelings of euphoria and relaxation. He said that it is a nice alternative to a cannabis high—more meditative and relaxed.

Harmala potentiates and enhances other entheogens. Ingesting a "potentiating" dose of harmala produces feelings of subtle energy flowing and a slight enhancement of perception.

Potentiating

Harmala is the main ingredient in the drink *yage*. It acts by potentiating the DMT, which is not normally active when taken orally. It works by inhibiting enzymes which normally destroy DMT in the stomach and by reducing the speed at which DMT is metabolized in the brain. Turner says, "A regular DMT experience can feel like some post-human identity in a distant galaxy aeons in the future. With harmala the experience gets linked through the individual identity to earth, humanity, and the evolutionary history stored within us."

Turner says that harmala can be used in combination with N,N—DMT, 5-MeO-DMT, LSD, psilocybin, and Ketamine with good results. However, he warns that harmala may be dangerous when combined with Ecstasy, mescaline and 2C-B.

Naranjo found harmaline to be hallucinogenic at dosage levels above 1 mg./kg. I.v. or 4 mg./kg. by mouth, which is about one half the threshold level for harmine. The onset of effects of harmaline or other derivatives is about one hour after ingestion by mouth, but almost instantaneous after intravenous injection. In this, harmaline resembles the chemically related tryptamines and differs from the slow-acting phenylethylamines.

Racemic tetra-hydroharmine, up to the amount of 300 mg. by mouth, was administered by Naranjo to a volunteer, who reported that at this dosage level there were subjective effects similar to those he experienced with 100 mg. of harmaline.

Ott's Ayahuasca Analogues.

8

Yage Visions

armala is the ingredient in the magic brew—*yage*—that acts as a catalyst to the entheogenic effects. The sense most consistently affected by harmaline is the visual. Shulgin says, "There can be vivid images generated, often in the form of meaningful dream-like sequences, and frequently containing subject matter such as wild animals and jungle scenes." Sometimes effects emerge as geometric patterns without much meaning; at other times visions with eyes closed have the character of mundane cartoonery.

A dark, quiet environment is generally preferrable. Pupil dilation is rare, but sharpened night vision is common, as William Emboden observes: "It has been demonstrated to the astonishment of foreigners that an Indian may run through a forest at night under the influence of the drug and not stumble or lose his footing. The vision is remarkably clear and the footing sure."

Ayahuasqueros describe long sequences of dream-like imagery; geometrical patterns; manifestations of spirit helpers, demons and deities; and tigers, birds and reptiles. They see dark-skinned men and women. They experience sensations of flying and of their own death; they see events at a great distance.

Many users claim that these visions appear in a spiritually significant progression. Luis told Weil that the stages become increasingly complex with practice and greater dosages: "First come patterns, then plants, then animals, then fantastic architecture and cities. If you are fortunate, you see "jaguars." Some claim that the ultimate experience is seeing into the eyes of "the veiled lady."

Americans who have experienced *yage* in the Amazon concur with these views. One woman said she "got only plants" until her fourth session. "Amazonian TV," as *yage* ingestion has been termed, is usually described as beautiful; even the lower-level phantasmagoria is regarded as basically enjoyable. However, more significant experiences are possible.

When Heinz Kusel drank the brew, he remarked, "There were two very definite attractions: I enjoyed the unreality of a created world. The images were not casual, accidental or imperfect, but fully organized to the last detail of highly complex, consistent, yet forever changing designs. They were harmonized in color and had a slick, sensuous, polished finish. The other attraction of which I was very conscious at the time was an inexplicable sensation of intimacy with the visions. They were mine and concerned only me. I remembered an Indian telling me that whenever he drank *ayahuasca,* he had such beautiful visions that he used to put his hands over his eyes for fear somebody might steal them. I felt the same way."

Heinz Kusel was told that the "aesthetic climax of the spectacle" was a vision of "the goddess with concealed eyes" (*I a diosa con los ojos vendados*), who dwelt inside the twining tropical vine." The first two times he tried *ayahuasca,* Kusel was disappointed. The third time "the color scheme became a harmony of dark browns and greens. Naked dancers appeared turning slowly in spiral movements. Spots of brassy lights played on their bodies which gave them the texture of polished stones. Their faces were inclined and hidden in deep shadows. "Their coming into existence in the center of the vision coincided with the rhythm of Nolorbe's song, and they advanced forward and to the sides, turning slowly. I longed to see their faces. At last the whole field of vision was taken up by a single dancer with inclined face covered by a raised arm. As my desire to see the face became unendurable, it appeared suddenly in full close-up with closed eyes. I know that when the extraordinary face opened them, I experienced a satisfaction of a kind I had never known."

Specificity of Yage Visions

The harmala alkaloids, with and without accompanying DMT-like compounds, have fascinated psychologists and others because of the unusual incidence of particular images. Outstanding in this regard are visions of tigers, snakes and naked women—often Negro. The color blue seems to predominate when *ayahuasca* is taken without additives.

Although this imagery is not universal, it is common—sometimes frightening—and is closely aligned to the archetypal symbolism that so fascinated Carl Jung. When Naranjo gave harmaline and harmine in psychotherapeutic settings to people who had never been in the jungle, he observed that much of the imagery that was aroused had to do with snakes, panthers, jaguars and other large felines. The recurrence of such images led him to speculate about the action of harmaline on "the collective unconscious."

The anthropologist Michael Harner is one of those claiming to have seen what the Indians are talking about, after having doubted throughout his year of study among the Jivaros of the Ecuadorian Amazon. He returned and was "turned on" to *yage* by another tribe. Marlene Dobkin de Rios recounts his experience: "For several hours after drinking the brew, Harner found himself, although awake, in a world literally beyond his wildest dreams. He met bird-headed people as well as dragon-like creatures who explained that they were the true gods of this world. He enlisted the services of other spirit helpers in attempting to fly through the far reaches of the Galaxy. He found himself transported into a trance where the supernatural seemed natural and realized that anthropologists, including himself, had profoundly underestimated the importance of the drug in affecting native ideology . . ."

Michael Harner and Claudio Naranjo made much of the "constancy" of both *yage* and harmaline visions in separate essays in *Hallucinogens and Shamanism.* A similar case has been put forth in Furst's *Flesh of the Gods,* where Gerardo Reichel-

Dolmatoff writes of the Tukano Indians of the western Amazon region of Colombia. These were the aboriginals Spruce first observed using yage. Koch-Grunberg described their *yage* practices: "According to what the Indians tell me, everything appears to be larger and more beautiful than it is in reality. The house appears immense and splendrous. A host of people is seen, especially women. The erotic appears to play a major role in this intoxication. Huge multicolored snakes wind themselves around the house posts. All colors are very brilliant . . ."

The Tukanos live in relative isolation. What caught the eye of Relchel-Dolmatoff was their use of representational paintings on house fronts, rattles and bark loincloths. The natives claimed that these designs were observed during *yage* inebriation. Relchel-Dolmatoff offered sheets of paper and a choice of twelve colored pencils to a number of adult males who frequently partook of the brew. "The men showed great interest in and concentration on this task and spent from one to two hours finishing each drawing."

Garden of Eden-type imagery is more specific to *yage* than any image pattern is to LSD, mescaline or psilocybin. The near-universality of many *yage* images suggests that these β-carbolines are a good deal closer than other psychedelics to being a "pure element" in a

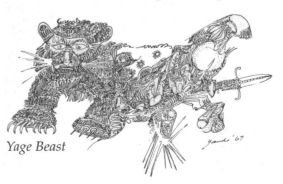

Yage Beast

Periodical Table of Consciousness. These β-carbolines, however, cannot be entirely "pure," as they are accompanied by many negative side-effects.

Auditory Component

Ingestion of *yage* often results in an enhancement of auditory acuity. To minimize distractions, urban users generally gather in the jungle at night, from about 8:00 p.m. to 2:00 a.m. rather than in someone's home. In *Wizard of the Upper Amazon,* Manuel Cordova-Rios described his frequent *ayahuasca* visions and stressed the improvement in his sense of hearing, which enlarged his understanding of jungle ways.

As with peyote, *Banisteriopsis* vines are known for "announcing themselves." Kusel writes, "Once a Campa Indian in my boat, when we were drifting far from shore, was called by *ayahuasca*, followed the call, and later emerged from the forest with a sampling of the fairly rare liana that today is cultivated by the *ayahuasquero* in secret spots. I myself certainly did not hear the call."

More typically, β-carbolines—like phenethlamines and psilocybian molecules—seem to inspire chants and singing. Weil took *yage* with Luis twice. About these experiences Weil says, "From time to time he would pick up a harmonica and turn into a one-man band. He would dance out the door and we would hear him chanting and singing off into the jungle . . . Victor and Luis sang and danced all night, periodically going out into the jungle to sing under the trees, then returning to the candle-lit house. Victor congratulated Luis on having made a really strong batch."

The Vine That Speaks

A *yagero's* chant is his most precious possession. It comes to him in dreams and stays with him all his life. Until a man receives his chant from the spirit of the vine, he cannot conduct ceremonies. Luis's chant was strangely hypnotic, a mixture of sounds, tunes and words. There were Spanish words, Ingano words and words of a sort I had never heard before. I asked him what one particular word meant. "It is *yage* speaking," he answered. "It doesn't mean; it is *yage* speaking.

—Andrew Weil

After Cordova-Rios became familiar with ayahuasca, he discovered that he could "direct," or at least greatly influence, resulting visions by songs and chants. This technique has been much used by native curanderos. Among some tribes, it is even said that "without singing, only visions of snakes appear."

Telepathic Element

Extrasensory perception is fairly prominent in the use of most entheogens. *Banisteriopsis* vines, throughout their history, have had an unusually high incidence of such effects, as reflected in the name given the first alkaloid isolated—"telepathine". The reports persist, despite the skepticism of many investigators. Schultes and Hofmann dismiss

these claims as "unfounded" in *Botany and Chemistry of Hallucinogens* .

In the *Journal of Psychoactive Drugs,* William
Burroughs expressed reservations about *yage*
having any exceptional telepathic properties:
"Medicine men use it to potentiate their powers, to
locate lost objects and that kind of thing. But I'm
not impressed much by their performance. Everybody has telepathic experiences all the time. These
things are not rare. It's just an integral part of life.
The faculty is probably increased to some extent
by any consciousness-expanding drug."

Flying and long-distance perceptions seem to be
characteristic of the telepathic element.
Villavicencio wrote, "As for myself, I can say for a
fact that when I've taken *ayahuasca* I've experienced dizziness, then an aerial journey in which I
recall perceiving the most gorgeous views, great
cities, lofty towers, beautiful parks, and other
extremely attractive objects."

Many natives claim not only to see, but to travel
great distances under the influence of *yage*, like
users of peyote and San Pedro. "Though he had
been no farther from his home than Mayoyoque,"
writes Weil, "Luis says that under *yage* he has left
his body and visited distant towns and cities,
including Florencia and Bogota."

Writing of *Banisteriopsis caapi* practices observed among the Cashinahua of Peru, anthropologist Kenneth Kensinger reported that "Informants
have described hallucinations about places far
removed, both geographically and from their own
experience. "Several, who have never been to or
seen pictures of Pucallpa, the large town at the
Ucayali River terminus of the Central Highway, have

described their visits under the influence of
ayahuasca to the town with sufficient detail for me
to be able to recognize specific shops and sights.

Citing an even more convincing instance,
Kensinger adds: "On the day following one
ayahuasca party, six of nine men informed me of
seeing the death of my chai, 'my mother's father.'
This occurred two days before I was informed by
radio of his death."

A similar experience was reported by Manuel
Cordova-Rios. After the most intense effects he'd
ever had on *yage*—he had seen his mother dying—he
returned to the home of his youth. There he
learned that she had died as he had "seen" it at just
that time.

In *Psychedelics: Their Uses and Implications*, by
Aaronson and Osmond, I describe a wonderfully
revitalizing experience engendered by an extraction
from this vine taken at an oasis near Las Vegas. I
made a visit to the craps tables toward the end of
the trip, where I had the astonishing feeling that I
could anticipate what was coming up on the dice as
bets were being placed.

Unfortunately, I hadn't really grasped the rules
of the game. What a classic dilemma! To know
something seemingly ESP, but being unsure of how
to play! This experience gave me an appreciation
of the "telepathine" nature of the experience.

Sexual Component

The sexual component is an ambiguous question.
Schultes and Hofmann discuss erotic usage of both
yage and Syrian rue in their many writings. Naranjo
was impressed by the archtypal sexual imagery

evoked by harmaline. Bigwood says that harmine, harmaline, ayahuasca, and DMT/harmaline are aphrodisiacs.

William Emboden adds that five milligrams of harmine alone produces measurable sexual activity in mice. This is doubtless one of the reasons why *ayahuasca* is used in coming of age ceremonies which sometimes involve flagellation and may be heavy in sexual content. He concludes that the psychoerotic effects of *ayahuasca* are well worth more careful documentation and attention

9

The Purgative Vine

age's taste does not cause as much gagging as peyote. However, the nausea in Andrew Weil's case was worse: "Vomiting is the first stage of the effect of *yage*. It is not fun, and I say that as someone who likes to vomit in certain circumstances. I held on to a tree and brought up a small quantity of intensely bitter liquid with wrenching spasms. *Yage* tastes much worse on the way up than on the way down—so bad that it left me shuddering for a few seconds . . . After a few minutes I had to answer another call of nature. The second action of *yage* is to purge the intestine. The effect is spectacular and painless. When I went back in, Luis asked me if it had been 'a good purge.' I told him yes. Eventually, he and Jorge also made trips to the jungle."

At first, Weil could swallow only two cups of *yage*, though he was encouraged to take more. Eventually he did get another cup down. "Luis," he reported, "wanted me to drink more of his brew,

but I could not." This element of the *yage* experience has been treated prominently in accounts
from other mind-explorers as well.

Yage concoctions are often referred to as a
purge, and *ayahuasca* has gained a reputation as
"the purgative vine." Harmaline and harmine by
themselves also bring about violent diarrhea and
vomiting in many users. Naranjo found that about
half of his harmaline subjects felt nausea, which he
attributed largely to "blocking attempts" to avoid a
full psychedelic experience.

Physical Side-Effects

Nausea, purges and retching are closely associated
with use of β-carbolines, but physical coordination
is otherwise hardly impaired. In most accounts, it
actually seems enhanced. When Weil met him, Luis
had been preparing *yage* weekly for curing sessions
for years, having first drunk it twenty-two years
earlier. Weil described Luis as youthful for his age,
a typical comment about *ayahuasqueros*, who have
been noted for possessing much energy and unusually smooth skin.

About the old man, Weil says, "In the course of
the evening Luis drank nine cups of the stuff. Each
one sent him to the jungle for further purging, but
his animated chanting continued without pause.
With each cup he became more energetic. Finally,
Jorge helped him into a heavy necklace of jaguar
teeth and a fantastic headdress of parrot feathers.
Then, palm-leaf rattles in his hands, Luis began a
stomping, turning dance around the house, all the
while uttering the sounds of *yage* . . . Luis went out
to vomit too but I could barely hear a break in his

chanting . . . He would dance out the door and we would hear him chanting and singing off into the jungle, circling the house, disappearing into the night. Then he would burst through the doorway in an explosion of feathers and palm leaves, growling like a jaguar."

Aside from the vomiting that frequently accompanies every cupful of the drink, the body's main physical responses include slight increases in blood pressure and heart rate—unless Daturas, Brugmansias or other scopolamine-containing substances have been added, which make the *yage* more dangerous. Some users feel a buzzing in the ears, prickling of the skin at the extremities, giddiness, profuse sweating or tremors. When Schultes first tried *yage*, he had severe diarrhea the following day.

Toxicity

Harmaline is about twice as toxic as harmine in most lab animals; the half-lethal dose—half the animals die—of harmine in dogs and mice is about 200 mg./kg. of body weight. No human deaths have been reported from these compounds. Weil writes: "Luis gives *yage* to anyone who wants it, to young and old, men and women, sick and well. He says it cannot hurt anyone, and though he gives it to pregnant women, young children and people with high fevers, no one suffers bad effects. Victor and he are both in good shape after taking enormous doses for years . . . And many of the patients say they are helped. I talked with people in Mayoyoque who say that visits to Luis cured them of various ills.

10

The Great Medicine

Yage is known as "the great medicine" in northwestern South America, where it is used for healing, much like peyote is used. Through its assumed intercession with spiritual entities, *yage* reveals the proper remedies or brings about healing spiritually or magically. In contrast to Western notions of medicine, *yage* is believed to be curative whether the patient or the healer swallows it. "Nature cures the disease," someone said, summing up these processes, "while the healer amuses the patient." Others speak of *ayahuaseros* as "singing the illness away."

In *Visionary Vine,* Marlene Dobkin de Rios outlined many of the procedures used in "curing sessions." In *Wizard of the Upper Amazo n,* Manuel Cordova-Rios gave another remarkable account. He continued to use *ayahuasca* medicinally when he returned to city life, seven years after his capture. "My cures," he comments, "for human ailments such as diabetes, hepatitis, leukemia, cancer, paralysis, rheumatism, epilepsy, suicidal depression and the dysfunctions of various internal organs have been called miraculous by some people."

Cancer Cure?

Donald Topping, Professor Emeritus of the University of Hawaii and President of the Drug Policy Forum of Hawaii, believes that *ayahuasca* is responsible for eradicating his cancer.

During my first session, "I saw a deep, black void. Nothing but darkness, which stayed in place for what seemed like minutes. All of the flashes, colors and forms disappeared while the blackness hovered over me. I sensed that it was death making its statement. It seemed to be saying, 'Yes, I'm here too, part of the system; but I'm not so bad, so don't be afraid.'"

"During the second trip I again felt the presence of the plant racing throughout my body, peeking and poking into every nook and cranny in search of something to work on, to straighten out, to put back in order, to polish. There was a definite presence, with similar shapes, colors and sounds. But unlike the first time, there was no message that I could discern. The plant was just busy doing its work."

Several months passed before Topping's next experience with *ayahuasca*. He followed a vegetarian diet and Chinese herbs, gradually regaining weight and strength "while the scars and soreness of the surgery were slowly healing." Topping decided to visit the plant again "to see if it had anything new to tell me, and to determine whether my first experience was delusional."

Topping reports, "Once again, after about fifteen minutes I began to notice the familiar rippling
effect. This time, however, the rippling quickly
turned into full-blown turbulence. As the images
and shapes began to appear, they had an air of joy
and exuberance. The serpents were smiling, the
jaguars laughing, and the giant birds swooped down
over me caressing with their outstretched wings. A
parade of persons, both known and unknown,
streamed by, each of them smiling and reaching to
touch me and tell by look that they loved me. As
the serpents and plants twisted and flashed before
me, they appeared to be smiling and reassuring me
that they had looked everywhere inside me, and
that everything was OK.

"Where was the darkness that I had experienced
before? Where was Mr. Death, I wondered? Then
suddenly, as though the plant heard my question, I
saw the void. Only this time it was clearly in the
background. It seemed to be peeping through the
montage of vibrant colors and forms, as though to
say, 'I'm still here, don't worry. It's not time for me
yet.' And then it faded away."

After a fourth session, Topping returned to his
oncologist for a blood test. The results showed
that his CEA count—the cancer activity indicator—
wasn't just normal, it was below normal!

When Topping told his doctor about his faith in
the medicinal plant used for centuries in the Amazon by shamans and healers, the doctor raised his
eyebrows, shrugged his shoulders, saying "You're
one of the lucky few."

"Lucky? Perhaps so", said Topping. "But to
dismiss my recovery against the odds as nothing
but luck is to ignore centuries of experience by

people who have learned to live with plants and understand them when they talk.

Purification

Topping offers his insights: "The most profound psychological change during my first experience occurred when I encountered death in the form of a soft, deep, dark void. The clear message was that death is always present, but nothing to be feared. It is there along with all the other forces and elements of nature, nothing exceptional. Death happens. Stating these obvious facts in words sound trite. But when the vine reveals such things, the impact is far more profound. Going into my first session the thought of imminent death, as predicted by my physician and the data, was a major concern. The vine put that to rest straight away.

"I do not believe that *ayahuasca* contains chemicals that destroy cancer cells like the chemotherapies do. That is not the way it works. Rather, *ayahuasca* serves to restore the normal, healthy alignment of cells while it seeks out and purges the aberrant ones that it finds while making its way throughout the body.. . .

"I cannot overstate the importance of the purge. This is the vine's way of eliminating physical as well as psychic toxins that don't belong inside a healthy body or mind. Although the cleansing itself is not pleasant, the lingering effects make it all worthwhile. It strikes me as a rite of purification."

Psychotherapeutic Potential

In *Visionary Vine*, Marlene Dobkin de Rios says "drug healing in the Peruvian jungle is a very old and honored tradition of dealing with psychological problems that predates Freudian analysis by centuries." Much of the treatment she enumerates is nonverbal. In some places, natives refer to *Banisteriopsis* as "the vine of death"—meaning that it causes a kind of ego death and rebirth.

Allen Ginsberg followed William Burroughs' path to South America to find *yage*. Ginsberg soon had a number of sessions—one of which produced the feeling that he was all covered with snakes; later he felt "like a snake vomiting out the universe." Ginsberg experienced the "vine of death." He wrote, "the whole fucking Cosmos broke loose around me, I think the strongest and worst I've ever had." He had fears that he might lose his mind.

An epilogue, written by Ginsberg, puts the experience in perspective: "Self deciphers this correspondence thus: the vision of ministering angels my fellow man and woman first wholly glimpsed while the *Curandero* gently crooned human in *ayahuasca* trance-state 1960 was prophetic of transfiguration of self consciousness from homeless mind sensation of eternal fright to incarnate body feeling present bliss now actualized 1963."

Transformative

Chilean psychiatrist Claudio Naranjo was among those fascinated by native use of psychoactive plants. Naranjo traveled into the Amazon taking along a Polaroid camera and blotter paper, on which he had drawn stars, the moon and the sun to mark different dosages of LSD. When he met some natives, he conveyed the idea that he was a "medicine man" and distributed the blotters, inviting the natives to try the star-doses, which were the lowest potency, while gazing at the night sky. Upon his return several days later, Naranjo learned that the natives liked his "medicine," considering it very powerful. In exchange, they gave him *ayahuasca*, which influenced his subsequent practice of psychotherapy. He described his using harmaline and harmine in *The Healing Journey*.

Naranjo summed up the quality of harmaline-aided psychotherapy in this way: "For one sharing the Jungian point of view, it would be natural to think of the artificial elicitation of archetypal experience as something that could facilitate personality integration, and therefore psychological healing. Yet the observation of the psychotherapeutic results of the harmaline experience was not the outcome of any deliberate attempt to test the Jungian hypothesis. These results came as a dramatic surprise . . . even before the recurrence of images became apparent . . ."

Naranjo continues, "It would be hard to offer a simple explanation for the instances of improvement brought about by the harmaline experience. Such improvement usually occurred spontaneously, without necessarily entailing insight into the particulars of the patient's life and conflicts. As in all cases of successful deep therapy, it did involve greater acceptance by the patients of their feelings and impulses and a sense of proximity to their self. Statements like these, however, are not very explicit, and only case histories can adequately illustrate . . ."

Enhancement of Relationships

A poignant example of the use of this vine's ability
to heal the relationship between a father and his
daughter is spelled out in the *MAPS Bulletin* published by the Multidisciplinary Association for
Psychedelic Studies.

Jack Lieberman and his 20-year-old daughter
Chloe participated in a ten-day experiential
Ayahuasca Healing Seminar in the Brazilian Amazon
led by Silvia Polivoy, a clinical psychologist practicing in Buenos Aires who had had extensive
shamanic training using various plant medicines.

About the experience, Jack wrote: "The more I
work with this medicine, the more experiences I
have of the divine . . . There is nothing like an
actual experience of divine presence to wake me up
to the fact that I am not in control of very much
that happens to me. I have been struggling with a
compulsion to control things for my entire 58
years. During an *ayahuasca* journey it became clear
to me that this need to control comes from a lack
of faith in the cosmic plan. It comes from fear and
the desire for self-protection from huge forces that
are beyond my control...."

Jack's plant teacher helped him relinquish some
of his control impulses in interactions with his
daughter and "spoke" to him during a journey after
he asked about how to handle fear. "That the
antidote to fear was faith and trust in the cosmic
drama taking place around me. Having faith does
not come easily for me. However, if I can see this
cosmic drama taking place, it is so much easier to
trust in the flow of the great river of the cosmos."

He received an important teaching from the plant that "concerned an addiction I have to thinking. I have been plagued by over-thinking most of my life, but until this recent journey I never framed it as an "addiction to thinking." The *ayahuasca* presence 'spoke' to me about this addiction and suggested tactics to use to deal with it. I was given the experience of how over-thinking feels, how debilitating it is, and that its first symptom is worry. By simply labeling worry as a symptom of an addiction that I want to be rid of, I have been able to make progress in not falling into what is essentially a bad habit."

About Chloe's account, she says, "Drinking ayahuasca in this fusion of past, present, and futuristic planes of reality, near my twentieth birthday and along with my dad, felt like a rite of passage. Rituals to acknowledge the beginnings and endings of stages in life are markedly absent from modern North American culture, and I didn't even realize the value of such a ritual until I was given the opportunity to experience one that was so appropriate for my own frame of reference. ...

I didn't drink *ayahuasca* to acknowledge my passage from childhood to adulthood, rather the ayahuasca showed me the significance of this passage. It let me in on some secrets of the universe that as a child I could not have fully understood... I observed the transfer of roles that is taking place in my father's life and in my own. Once I was a helpless infant, relying completely on my parents. Now we live independently, and in the future my dad will return to an infantile state and I, fully grown, will care for him. This is intellectually obvious, but with *ayahuasca* I did not simply know it, I experienced it....

Chloe continues, "The experience established us as two sovereign individuals, separate spiritual peers. It became easier to get along (with my father) because I understood where he was coming from more deeply, and was able to interact with more honesty and less attachment."

Healing Churches

At the end of the 20th Century, the religious use of the tea spread throughout Brazil, giving rise to churches in many of the major cities. These churches have become well-known for their work in helping people to effectively overcome alcohol and drug addiction.

The Santo Daime religion, one of the three major *ayahuasca* "cults", was founded in the early part of the 20th Century by a seven-foot-tall black man, near the border with Bolivia and Peru, after he had been introduced to an *ayahuasca* drink. During a retreat in the forest, Master Irineu, as he later came to be called, received visions of the Virgin Mary in the form of the Queen of the Forest, who revealed to him a religious doctrine which he was to bring to the world through the specific rituals that she showed him.

Gradually Master Irineu gathered a group of people around him and started to receive hymns "from the astral plane," which became an integral part of the rituals which they practice. An observer of these rites comments: "The doctrine which is revealed in [these hymns] is a Christian doctrine blended with the native religions, with a profound reverence for Mother Nature, especially the forest, personified as the Virgin Mary."

Ayahuasca Healing Ceremony

Visionary Vine

11

Brew Preparation

 yrian Rue seeds are ground in a cof-
fee-type grinder and the powder put
into gelatine capsules. Such capsules
take about two hours after ingestion
for the harmala to take effect. Sometimes the
powder is boiled for a few minutes to make a bitter
tea, which takes about an hour to come on. Turner
suggests spreading consumption of Syrian Rue over
an hour to reduce stomach disturbances.

Approximately three grams, or 1 1/4 teaspoons
of finely ground Syrian Rue seed is required for a
potentiating dose. A larger dose is best avoided
because it will only increase nausea without increasing the potentiating effect.

Harmala extract causes less nausea. It can be
extracted by using vodka as a solvent. An advantage of extraction is that it can be smoked, which
produces a nice high and comes on within minutes.
Smoking is not as long-lasting as ingestion, however.

Yage Brew Dosage

Four or five half-foot pieces of bark from a me-
dium-sized inch-or-two thick vine are often provided per person in *yage* brews. Estimates of dosages presented here are rough, being generally
based on experiences in the field rather than in the
laboratory.

Villalba saw natives use about 20 cm. of the
stem, which Hoffer and Osmond estimated as
containing about 0.5 gm. of β-carboline alkaloids.
"Under its influence," they wrote, "they jumped,
screamed, and ran about wildly but continued to
take it for days to maintain the state of excitation."
Villalba tried the concentrated liquid and had no
reaction, whereupon he concluded that other white
people who had seen visions of the future were
exaggerating the effect.

Michael Valentine Smith, in *Psychedelic Chemistry*, reports that harmaline and harmine are both
active at about 200 mg. oral dosage. Bigwood
disputes this, saying that to get effective potentiation from the hydrochloride salts an adult should
swallow at least 300 mg. harmaline or 500 mg.
harmine. Shulgin puts the effective dose range of
harmaline at 70 to 100 mg. intravenously or 300 to
400 mg. orally. *Legal Highs* by Gottlieb states as its
rough estimate that the equivalent of 100 mg.
harmine is "50 mg. harmaline, 35 mg.
tetrahydraharmine, 25 mg. harmolol or harmol, and
4 mg. methoxy-harmalan."

Preparation

In the preparation of *yage*, appropriate Banisteriopsis vines are generally cut into 6- to 8-inch pieces. The bark is then pounded or shaved off and either soaked in cold water or boiled for hours, sometimes a full day, usually with one or more admixtures. Boiling produces a brown or reddish-brown concoction that's bitter and salty; boiled ayahuasca is said to cause nausea to a greater degree than the cold-water infusion. The usual course is to drink a couple of cupfuls, which produce an experience lasting three or four hours. Then, if desired, more *yage* may be drunk.

When it is boiled, the bark has a light chocolate or reddish color with a slight greenish tinge. Villalba noted that standing *yage* changed "to a topaz color with a bluish green fluorescence." After six or seven experiences of the cold water infusion, as prepared in the Colombian Amazon, Schultes judged the effects as differing little "from those from the boiled concoction used in the Putumayo. The intoxication is longer in setting in, and much more of the drink must be taken, but the symptoms of the intoxication and their intensity seem to me to be very similar."

Onset

Harmaline, when taken orally by itself, takes a comparatively long time to prompt psychological effects—often about two hours. Potions containing both DMT-like and harmala alkaloids, however, take effect rapidly. Spruce noticed responses from yage within two minutes, an unusually quick onset from oral ingestion; others have observed initial effects taking hold within five minutes. Contrasting the slow onset of harmaline alone against his ayahuasca experiences and his harmaline/DMT experiences, Bigwood says that the latter are almost identical as far as the time course and visual effect—they both come on quite rapidly.

Admixtures

Jeremy Bigwood found in the course of experimentation that DMT could be made orally active in doses of 100 mg. when combined with a sub-threshold dose of harmaline. Many reports from natives indicate that the addition of certain leaves—almost all containing DMT-like substances—makes the *yage* visions "brighter." Investigators almost unanimously agree that significant potentiation occurs when β-carbolines and short-acting tryptamines are mixed together.

The adding of DMT-containing leaves to "brighten" the visions complicates this matter further. *Psychotria viridis* is the most common additive, but *Diplopterys* leaves are said to be 5-10 times more alkaloid-rich than an equivalent amount of *Psychotria*—so fewer of these leaves are used. There is a vast range of propellants for this kind of shamanic soul flight.

While β-carbolines are essential to the psychoactivity of *yage*, the tryptamines are most important in producing the mental effects. The harmala alkaloids enable DMT-like substances to become active to produce synergistic effects. Schultes and Hofmann, commenting on the expanded length and vividness of results when DMT-like compounds are included, indicate how important in terms of color the presence of monoamine oxidase inhibitors can be: "Whereas visions with the basic drink are seen usually in blue, purple, or gray, those induced when the tryptaminic additives are used may be brightly colored in reds and yellows."

Major Additives

Malouetia tamaquafina;

A species of Tabermaemontana of the Apocynaceae;

Acanthaceous Teliostachya lanceolata var. crispa or Toe Negra;

Calathea veitchiana of the Maranthaceae;

Amaranthaceous Alternanthera lehmannii;

A species of Iresine;

Ferns including Lygodium venustum and Lomariopsis japurensis; Phrygylanthus Eugenioides of the Mistletoe family;

The mint Ocimum micranthum;

A species of the sedge genus Cyperu;

Cacti including species of Opuntia and Epiphyllum;

A member of the genus Clusia of the Guttiferae.

Ayahuasqueros often include at least one additive to *yage* infusions to enhance states of mind brought about by *B. caapi, inebrians* and *quitensis.* In Colombia, Daturas and closely related species of *Brugmansia* are sometimes used. They undoubtedly give this drink added kick but are dangerous. Often tobacco is added. Major additives are listed by Schultes and Hofmann in the Table below.

The main additives are *Psychotria carthaginensis, P. viridis, Tetrapterys methystica* and *Banisteriopsis rusbyana.* Leaves and stems of the last, known as *oco-yage* or *chagrapanga,* don't contain the β-carboline alkaloids produced by *B. caapi* and *inebrians.* Instead, they have a large amount of N, N-DMT, 5-methoxy-N,N-DMT, 5-hydroxy-N,N-DMT and N-β-methyltetrahydro-β-carboline. The other added species contain DMT-type compounds, rendered orally active by the harmala compounds in *ayahuasca.*

Bark of the Vine

Essential to any *yage* concoction is bark from specific *Banisteriopsis* vines—generally *B. caapi,* often *B. inebrians* and sometimes *B. quitensis. B. caapi* climbs up tropical forest trees until its flowers are exposed to direct sunlight. It is so greedy for sunlight that sometimes it eventually kills supporting trees. It is occasionally started in greenhouses, where it has been known to take over the roof. The flowers are small and pink, much like apple blossoms. At its base, the vine often has a diameter of six inches.

Avoid MAO Inhibitors

A major component of *ayahuasca* is a monoamine inhibitor which acts to quell a key enzyme in the body responsible for processes in the brain and throughout the body. Severe negative reactions due to the use of certain foods or prescription medications can occur. Therefore, it is generally recommended that one not eat anything prior to this vine's usage—especially an antidepressant like Prozac or its analogs, or amphetamines, or antihistamines.

Aged cheeses, beer, yeast extract, pineapples, soy sauce, wine, cream, avocados, bananas, coffee, liver, figs, sauerkraut, raisins, yogurt or pickled herring should never be eaten prior to drinking *yage*. Use of mescaline, cocaine, heroin, Ecstasy or 2C-B, or any phenethylamines with *yage* should be avoided.

In some tribes, stringent dietary procedures are practiced for up to two weeks before ingestion of *ayahuasca*, although many natives use it weekly. Peruvians getting *yage* from healers commonly abstain from salt, lard, sweets and sometimes sex a day before and a day after taking an infusion. Such procedures help to minimize nausea, but they certainly don't eliminate it. Weil was advised not to eat anything before noon; he hadn't eaten since breakfast the evening he received *yage* from Luis.

12

Ayahuasca Botany

 armala alkaloids (or β-carbolines) are manufactured by plants in at least eight botanical families, including tobacco. Oscar Janiger and Marlene Dobkin de Rios report that about 10 to 20 mcg. harman and norharman have been detected in smoke from a single cigarette, or forty to a hundred times that found in the tobacco leaf.

Botanical understanding of what causes *yagé* effects has been, as Schultes put it, more "fraught with confusion" than is the case with other entheogens. Schultes and Hofmann described these confusions almost apologetically, writing that "It is difficult for the nonbotanist to understand our lack of understanding of specific delimitations of drug plants, the use of which has been known for more than a century."

Natives distinguish at least six different botanical sources of *ayahuasca*. Two that are said to be the most powerful may not yet have been adequately described—botanically or chemically.

These vines have become relatively rare in their native jungle growing area, so genuine *yage* is rarely seen. Several people who have searched for the vine report that a decent *ayahuasquero* is hard to find these days because many have given in to "alcohol abuse."

Richard Spruce set identification efforts off to a bad start by suggesting that *yage's* peculiar qualities were from the roots of "painted *caapi.*" This was a vine he called *Haemadictyon amazonicum,* of which no known other example exists than what he collected since assigned to the Prestonia genus. Although he said that the Indians considered a *Banisterlopsis* vine an essential ingredient, his misdirection was repeated by others.

Banisteriopsis caapi

The Colombian chemist Fischer, isolating the first alkaloid in *yage,* placed it in the Aristolochia genus. *Banisteriopsis caapi* first became known as a main source when French pharmacologists Perrot and Harriet reviewed this psychoactive complex in terms of its botany and chemistry.

This magic inebriant, which many northwest-ernmost South American Indians believe frees the soul "from corporeal confinement,"

Cultivated Banisteriopsis caapi *shoots branching out in all directions.*

R.E. Schultes:Harvard Botanical Museum

appears in a wide range of forms that are significantly distinct in their effects. When *Banisteriopsis caapi* and *B. inebrians* take root, they are hardy and can attain great heights. While frequently cultivated in South America, they have been grown only rarely in U.S. greenhouses.

"The natives often have special names for diverse 'kinds' of Ayahuasca," write Schultes and Hofmann in *Plants of the Gods*, "although the botanist frequently finds them all representative of the same species. It is usually difficult to understand the aboriginal method of classification: some may be age forms; others may come from different parts of the liana vine; still others may be ecological forms growing under varying conditions of soil, shade, moisture, etc. The natives assert that these 'kinds' have a variety of effects and it is conceivable that they may actually have different chemical compositions."

Syrian Rue

The most concentrated source of harmala alkaloids is the seed of *Peganum harmala*, commonly known as Syrian rue. The seeds contain from 2% to 7% mixed harmala alkaloids. It is a small bushy shrub that has been used traditionally for psychoactive effects. Known from antiquity, this species belongs to the Zygophyllaceae family rather than to the Malpighiaceae family to which the *Banisteriopsis* species belong. It grows some three feet high in desert habitats, has leaves cut into long, narrow segments and produces small, white flowers.

Although Syrian rue is native only to Central Asia and Syria, it has migrated and grows wild

Syrian rue is a botanical source of harmala alkaloids

along the Mediterranean coasts of Europe, Africa and the Middle East. Syrian rue is esteemed from Asia Minor across to India and northeast Tibet. Its bitter, brown seeds contain β-carbolines identical to those in entheogenic *Banisteriopsis* vines and in about the same proportions.

Syrian rue has been employed in folk medicine as well as being used for dyes in Turkish and Persian rugs. Among Egyptians and a few other peoples, the dried seeds have long been associated with preparation of a love potion—despite the nauseating effects common to most harmala alkaloids. David Flattery brought attention to this shrub in a published doctoral dissertation entitled *Huoma,* in which he theorizes, almost entirely on linguistic grounds, that *P. harmala* was the "Huoma" or "Soma" of ancient Persia and India.

13
Ayahuasca Chemistry*

 armala alkaloids or β-carbolines are an entheogenic compound-cluster with three-ringed molecules. Harmaline is the most significant of these compounds tested. Its formal names are 4,9-dihydro-7-methoxy-l-methyl-3H-pyrido-[3,4-b] indole and 7-methoxy-l-methyl-3,4-dihydro-β-carboline. This compound-cluster exhibits an extra ring attached to its basic indolic chemical structure. The resulting three-ring β-carboline system has an unusually placed methoxy (CH_3O) group, which Alexander Shulgin points out is in marked contrast to the orientation found in serotonin and the related tryptamines.

Fischer assayed *yage*, isolating an alkaloid that he named "telepathine". Barriga-Villalba and Albarracin isolated two alkaloids from this drink that they named "yajeine" and "yajeinine". Lewin isolated banisterine, and Wolfes, as well as Rumpf and Elger, asserted that all these alkaloids were identical—they were harmaline, an indole derivative found in seeds and roots of Syrian rue—*Peganum harmala.* Subsequently Chen and Chen, working with clearly identified botanicals, demonstrated that all these substances were harmaline.

Hochstein and Paradies determined that results from ingestion of *yage,* without other botanical additives, came mainly from interaction of three molecules—harmaline, harmine and d-1,2,3,4-tetra-hydroharmine.

One wonders how peoples in primitive societies, with no knowledge of chemistry or psychology, ever hit upon a solution to the activation of an alkaloid by a monoamine oxidase inhibitor.

—Richard Evans Schultes

By gentle oxidation, harmaline is converted into harmine, the other main psychoactive constituent in the botanicals. Upon reduction, harmaline yields d-1,2,3,4-tetrahydroharmine, a third but minor contributor.

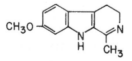

Harmaline
(4,9-dihydro-7-methoxy-1-methyl-3H-pyrido-[3,4-b]-indole,
or 7-methoxy-1-methyl-3,4-dihydro- β-carboline)

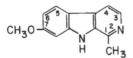   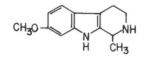

Harmine   *d-1,2,3,4-Tetrahydroharmine*

Harmaline and harmine are both crystalline, the first appearing as yellow and the second as green hydrochloride salts. According to Hoffer and Osmond, both form these salts "with one equivalent of acid. Harmine crystallizes in needles, melting point 256-257 degree C., harmaline in platelets, melting point 238 degree *C. Harmine* is slightly soluble in water, alcohol, chloroform, and ether. Its hydrochloride salt is freely soluble in hot water. Harmaline is slightly soluble in hot alcohol and dilute acids, and forms blue fluorescent solutions."

A number of other β-carboline alkaloids have been developed in the laboratory. Michael Valentine Smith describes the preparation of several analogs in his *Psychedelic Chemistry*. The 6- or 10-methoxy isomer of harmaline, sometimes known as 10-methoxy-harmalan, is about half again as potent by weight as harmaline.

Natural in Humans

At least one harmala alkaloid is present in the pineal gland of humans, as well as in that of several animals. Interestingly, this compound is more abundant in the pineal glands of highly advanced yogis, according to some reports, which has led to speculation that its presence may impart power to the "third eye" in mid-forehead, where the pineal gland lies.

Discussing harmaline's effectiveness in psycho-therapy, Naranjo writes: "I want to mention that this alkaloid is of special interest because of its close resemblance to substances derived from the pineal gland of mammals. In particular, 10-meth-oxy-harmaline, which may be obtained in vitro from

the incubation of serotonin in pineal tissue, resembles harmaline in its subjective effects and is of
greater activity than the latter. This suggests that
harmaline (differing from 10-methoxy-harmaline
only in the position of the methoxy group) may
derive its activity from the mimicry of a metabolite
normally involved in the control of states of consciousness."

Bo Holmstedt, a pioneer in research on harmala
alkaloids from the Karolinska Institutet in Sweden,
suggested that similar substrates and enzymes are
in the pineal gland for endogenous production of
DMT, 5-methoxy-DMT and the N-methyl analogs of
harmine and harmaline. Brimblecombe and Pinder
discuss in *Hallucinogenic Agents* the possible metabolism routes by which adrenoglomerulotropine
and melatonin, normally present in the pineal body,
may be turned into 6-methoxy-harmalan. However,
no evidence has conclusively shown that this con-
version actually takes place in the human brain.

As with DMT, theories have been advanced that
schizophrenia is associated with increased production of harmala alkaloids. As Shulgin remarked,
consensus among researchers now is that this
hypothesis is "a red herring."

14

Ibogaine*

bogaine is found in the roots of *Tabernanthe iboga* of equatorial Africa. It is the most studied of the alkaloids in the root and is representative of another cluster of indolic molecules. Ibogaine is a naturally-occurring compound of special interest because it comes from an entirely different botanical family from those discussed so far.

Some commentators credit wild boars with inspiring the practice of ingesting bark from the roots of the "iboga," "eboga," "boga," "libuga," "bocca," "eboga," "leboga" or "lebuga" plant. When boars dig up and eat roots of the shrub they go into a frenzy, jumping around wildly. Similar reports have been made about porcupines and gorillas.

Griffon du Bellay brought specimens of *T. iboga* to Europe in 1864. He stated that when the yellowish root of this plant is eaten, "it is not toxic except in high doses in the fresh state. In small quantities, it is an aphrodisiac and a stimulant of the nervous system; warriors and hunters use it constantly to keep themselves awake during night watches."

Use of shavings from the root of *iboga* is widespread in Gabon and adjacent parts of the Congo. Natives use it during lion hunts to remain awake and alert for up to two days while waiting for the cats to cross their path. According to some residents of Gabon, colonial Germans permitted—and possibly encouraged—use of *iboga* to suppress fatigue among workers on the construction of the Douala-Yaounde railroad and other projects.

Dybowski and Landrin coined the name ibogaine when they extracted the major alkaloid in the root bark in the early 19th Century. They reported it to be almost as psychoactive in isolation as the entire root. Chemical studies have confirmed that it is a central nervous system stimulant. The root's consciousness-changing effects were not analyzed by Western scientists until the mid-1950s, however.

The earliest written report indicating consciousness changing effects came in 1903 from J. Guien described the experience of an initiate in a cult in the Congo. "Soon all his sinews stretch out in an extraordinary fashion. An epileptic madness seizes him, during which, unconscious, he mouths words, which when heard by the initiated ones, have a prophetic meaning and prove that the fetish has entered him."

Iboga, like peyote and *ayahuasca*, is often used as a religious sacrament. Bwiti (male) and Mbiri (female) *iboga*-using cults in the Congo and Gabon, which have grown to several million members, conduct their ceremonies at night amidst dancing and drumming. As with *yage, iboga* root scrapings are employed to evoke communication with deceased ancestors.

Few people outside of Africa have had access to the botanical source or to synthesized ibogaine. People who try ibogaine tend to be impressed; a few have not, considering this cluster merely composed of stimulants like amphetamine.

Botany

The *Tabernanthe iboga* bush, which grows to about five-feet high, is common in the equatorial underforests in the western part of Africa. It is one of at least seven species of this genus—two of which are known to have been used as mind-alterers. The other is *T. manii.*

One of the mysteries about *Tabernanthe*, say Schultes and Hofmann, "is why the Apocynaceae, probably the family richest in alkaloids, should be so sparingly represented in the list of species valued and utilized for their psychotomimetic properties." They suggest that there are undoubtably sundry species in this family possessing organic constituents capable of inducing visual or other hallucinations, but that these either have not been discovered by aborigines or are too toxic for human consumption.

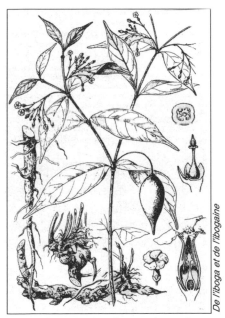

Tabernanthe iboga, *the major source of ibogaine and related alkaloids.*

De l'iboga et de l'ibogaine

Roots similar to those of *Rauwolfia* form from a bulbous mass, which can grow to about four-inches across. Individual roots branch off from this mass in all directions and may extend as far as 32-inches.

The stems, which are said to have a vile odor, contain small amounts of ibogaine and related alkaloids along with large amounts of latex.

Chemistry

Ibogaine was isolated in 1901 from *Tabernanthe iboga* roots by Dybowski and Landrin, and by Haller and Heckel. The most abundant alkaloid in the shrub's root bark, ibogaine, exhibits the indole nucleus structure common to most entheogens. Its stereochemistry—the dotted lines are at angles to the rest of the molecule—was established in the late 1960s.

At least twelve *iboga* alkaloids are known and appear in about the same proportion in both *T. iboga* and *T. manii*. They are all similar in structure to ibogaine. The most important are tabernanthine, ibogamine, coronaridine, voacangine, isovacangine and conopharyngine. Their structures are described in Hoffer and Osmond's *The Hallucinogens*.

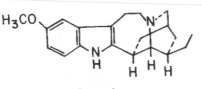

Ibogaine

P.B. Schmidt studied the effects of ibogaine homologs in humans and reported on doses of 0.1 to 1.2 mg./kg. of ibogaine hydrochloride administered orally to twelve subjects. It produced states of inebriation and mild sedation with minor psychic changes. The dosage used by Schmidt may have been insufficient, however, to bring on ibogaine's full effects.

Physical Effects

Moderate doses of ibogaine or *iboga* root bark are stimulating—much like amphetamine—and act as a choline-esterase inhibitor, causing some hypertension and stimulation of digestion and appetite. As with harmala alkaloids, there is no pupil dilation.

In high doses, it can cause nervous excitment, mental confusion and a general state of drunkenness. In large amounts, these compounds induce nausea and vomiting and put users into a trance where engaging in physical activity is difficult. In excessive amounts, *iboga* ingestion leads to convulsions, paralysis and even death brought on by arrest of respiration. Generally the inebriation so interferes with motor activity that the initiates can only sit gazing into space. During the comatose period the soul is sometimes believed to leave the body to wander in search of one's ancestors.

On a number of occasions, leaders of the Bwiti religion have been brought before courts on charges of murder because death has occured during initiations. Such an instance happened in the 1950s when they were accused of administering large amounts of *T. iboga* to a young boy for purposes of acquiring his cadaver. Apparently panther whiskers were mixed into the concoction. In *Flesh of the Gods*, James Fernandez reports that most such cases of suspected murder involve "women or young people of small physical stature."

Sexual Enhancement

Ibogaine can deepen the sexual drive so that one experiences a simultaneous sense of detachment and involvement that is empowering, according to Terence McKenna. It seems to function much as *ayahuasca* does to become a boundary-dissolving visionary entheogen. McKenna suggests that research is needed to determine if ibogaine can impact sexual dysfunction.

Mental Effects

James Fernandez, writing about *iboga* in Furst's *Flesh of the Gods*, drew on accounts from some sixty users, most of whom spoke of the experience as a journey. As Bwiti initiates, they communed with ancestors, who mostly appeared white—a color signifying death to natives. *Iboga* is intimately associated with death.

The plant is often anthropomorphized as a supernatural being that can carry one away to the realm of the dead. Sorcerers take the drug to seek information from the spirit world. A feeling of levitation is common. Seeing rainbow-like halos is a sign that one is approaching the land of the ancestors and gods.

Time perception is altered so that time is lengthened. Initiates often feel that their spiritual trip has taken many hours or even days. Large doses induce auditory, olfactory and gustatory synesthesia. The initiate's mood can vary from fear to euphoria.

Fernandez noted similarities in visionary elements. Typically, native users see a crowd of black men who had not eaten *eboka* and were unable to pass to the beyond; then they are met by a relative who is white and guides the user over rivers and other obstacles, traveling on "a journey down a long road that eventually leads to great powers."

Often the user meets other ancestors in order of descent, going further and further back in lineage. Sometimes the journey ends in the middle of a rainbow. Time perception may have been lengthened so initiates feel that they had been traveling in the spirit world for several days.

Ndong Asseko, age twenty-two, unmarried and a member of the Essabam clan. reports, "When I ate *eboka* I found myself taken by it up a long road in a deep forest until I came to a barrier of black iron. At that barrier, unable to pass, I saw a crowd of black persons also unable to pass. In the distance beyond the barrier it was very bright. I could see many colors in the air but the crowd of black people could not pass.

"Suddenly my father descended from above in the form of a bird. He gave to me then my

eboka name, Onwan Misengue, and enabled me to fly up after him over the barrier of iron. As we proceeded the bird who was my father changed from black to

At the end of her initiation, waiting for her ancestors to arrive.

Flesh of the Gods

white—first his tail feathers, then all his plumage. We came then to a river the color of blood in the midst of which was a great snake of three colors— blue, black, and red. It closed its gaping mouth so that we were able to pass over it."

The aim of the experience is for members to achieve a state of "one-heartedness"—*n1em mvore*— in the early hours of the morning, when the spirits of the initiates and ancestors have mingled. Afterwards, there is a large communal meal.

Being fairly puritanical, the Bwiti religion re-gards aphrodisiacal effects as antithetical to the religious purpose of *iboga*. Many reports, however, emphasize the erotic component of the ibogaine experience. According to Adam Gottlieb in *Sex Drugs and Aphrodisiacs*: "It is also used as an aphrodisiac and cure for impotence. Its efficacy as a sex drug is borne out by my personal experience and that of others."

There have been extensive animal studies with ibogaine. When many species are given large amounts, animal subjects appear frightened and act as though they are hallucinating. Hoffer and Osmond have summarized much of this work in *The Hallucinogens.*

American Use

Use of ibogaine in the U.S. has been limited. In *Sky Cloud Mountain*, Walter Anirman describes his experience, which involved two trips similar to accounts from African natives:

"My head prismed with colors that resolved themselves into eidetic, omnisensual scenes of long forgotten times.

"I was ten years old again and running down the railroad tracks near home, off with my boyhood companions into another day of adventures. The tracks became silver cords weaving a Turk's head knot around me, then straightened and became the implacable bars of a crib where I—a diapered baby—howled to be free. The colors turned red, crimson, scarlet, purple; became bright liquids flowing as blood in my sentient tubeways, oozing nourishment through flesh, pulsing with a million aspects of life.

"Occasionally, the visionary onslaught would ease for a moment, and I would awaken to my body crumpled on a blanket in a magically unfocusable forest. I managed to sit up several times, hoping to channel the energy more directly along my spine, but could never hold it, and fell over. No sooner was I down than I was off once more, foraging through luxurious strata of psyche, meeting myself in mirrors of mind, abbreviating time to dally with images of yesterday as real in recall as they had been in reality."

Psychotherapeutic Use

When long past childhood experiences can be so vividly relived, ibogaine's psychotheraputic possibilities become intriguing. In *The Healing Journey* Claudio Naranjo explored ibogaine's psychotherapeutic efficacy. fifty treatments he witnessed or knew about indirectly.

With no drug have I witnessed such frequent explosions of rage as with this particular one. With ibogaine, anger is not directed to the present situation, but, rather, to persons or situations in the patient's past, toward whom and by which it was originally aroused. This is in accord with the general tendency for the person under ibogaine to become concerned with childhood reminiscences and fantasies.

There is a great difference between the domain of past experience to which MDA facilitates the access and that which is exposed by means of ibogaine. Whereas with the former it is a matter of events being remembered, and perhaps reactions or feelings in the face of such events, with ibogaine it is a world of fantasies that the person meets. Parental images evoked by means of ibogaine probably correspond to the child's conception of his parents, which still lies in the subconscious of the adult — but these do not necessarily match the parent's reality. The therapeutic process with ibogaine may be depicted as that of seeing such constructions for what they are and being freed through confrontation with them....

—Claudio Naranjo

Fights Chemical Addictions

Toward the end of the 20th Century, Howard Lotsof, who had become addicted to heroin in the early 1960s, while seeking a new kind of "high" stumbled upon a dose of ibogaine, and found to his surprise that this substance seemed to free him from his addiction. Impressed by the effect, he gave ibogaine to six friends also "in the arms of Morpheus." Five of the six reported that they overcame their heroin addiction to a large extent.

Lotsof pursued this matter doggedly over the years. Because ibogaine is on Schedule I of the U.S. Federal drug laws—meaning that it is illegal and carries maximum sentencing—he established several centers overseas to treat alcohol and opiate addictions with ibogaine. Over the last couple of decades of the 20th Century, Lotsof received four patents for analogs that are found in the *Tabernathe Iboga* plant, and developed a product—EndAbuse—that has become popular as a treatment for drug and alcohol abuse.

Largely through the instigations of Lotsof, a number of studies have been conducted—mainly in Amsterdam and St. Kitts—and a voluminous "Ibogaine Dossier" has been assembled and can be found on the internet. In 1999 an International Ibogaine Conference was held at the New York University School of Medicine. The findings from this research on addiction and withdrawal suggest that effects of the treatments lessen within about six months, except in those cases where the treatment was coupled with psychotherapy.

Resets Behavior Patterns

The drug-complex seems to arouses early life traumas in those who use it and seems to compliment Jankov's "Primal Scream" method of psychotherapy. Subsequent use of ibogaine seems to work only a few times, with optimum results achieved in those over the age of 35. However almost all who have experienced ibogaine seem to reset former abberent behavior patterns.

An example of such recovery is provided by Sophia F., who guides others in these experiences. She had three sessions that were all very different. The first was 5 mg./kg., the second 6.5 mg./kg. and the third was 11 mg./kg. Her intent in the first session was to see if she could connect "with any kind of memory with my birth mother, because I was adopted." Curious, she also wanted to see if ibogaine could take her back to any past life experience. Much to her astonishment, she learned about the tremendous lack of bonding she had had with her adoptive mother.

Revisiting Mother

I went back to being with my adopted mother as an infant while she was holding me. My head was bobbing, my nose was banging into her neck . . . then I smelled her, and it didn't feel right. I was trying to get away because it didn't smell right . . . That's where I realized I retreated into myself . . .

For the first time, I really experienced that lack of bonding, and why it never occurred. She didn't smell right, and there was no connection.

I found myself asking the question: "Can I remember my birth mother?" Soon I was back in this other experience in which I was totally merged into another being. And I could feel this woman's tenderness. I could feel her sadness and it was my sadness. It was a sadness I have felt throughout my life.

And then I would go from that to my adopted mother, and the bobbing, and back and forth between the feelings of discomfort with her and the feeling of being me with my natural mother. After a while of going back and forth between the two feelings, I felt "Okay, I think I've got it now! I think I've got it. I see now how this all got started."

—Sophia F.

15

Preparing Ibogaine

abernanthe iboga is grown mainly in Gabon and the Congo, although it can be cultivated in most tropical and semitropical areas. What little has been raised in the U.S. has largely been propagated in greenhouses.

Frequently cultivated in villages of Gabon as a decorative shrub, *iboga* produces a yellowish- or pinkish-white flower, which grows from the same point as pairs of leaves and branches. The plant yields a small, oval, yellowish-orange fruit — about the size of an olive with an edible sweet pulp — which doesn't contain ibogaine but has sometimes been used as a medicine "for barrenness in women."

Natives generally rasp off the root bark and then eat it as a dried powder. Sometimes the powder is mixed with water and drunk as a beverage. *Iboga* is stronger in its fresh state. In a few places, it is taken with other plants, especially with *Alchornea floribunda*, which is also considered an aphrodisiac, or with marijuana.

Synthesization for use among the psychedelic subculture is rare. Ibogaine is a Schedule I drug in federal law. Its illegal status and the difficult manufacturing process have led most psychedelic chemists to conclude, as Michael Valentine Smith suggests in *Psychedelic Chemistry,* that it's concoction isn't worth the trouble.

Dosage

The bark from the roots, especially the smaller ones, is preferred by the natives. It is yellowish-brown in its fresh state and turns gray when dried. Alkaloids constitute up to 2.5 percent of the roots and may total more than 6 percent of the root bark.

Native *iboga* cults generally use two or three teaspoons of the dried, powdered root bark for women and three to five for men. At this dosage the results are not primarily mental but do excite a substantial activation of motor response, which considerably assists drumming and dancing. Users feel light, almost as if they are walking above the ground. Naranjo found that a third of his ibogaine subjects felt a desire to move or dance during their sessions.

Sometimes a third to a full kilogram of the root bark is ingested in initiation ceremonies. In order to enter the Bwiti cult, an initiate has to see Bwiti, a vision which can only be attained by eating sufficient quantities of *iboga.*

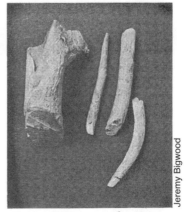

Roots of Tabernanthe iboga.

Jeremy Bigwood

The ritual starts early in the morning, with the root bark being eaten throughout the day "to break open the head" and establish communication with Bwiti and ancestors. By evening the visionary state is usually achieved, when all members of the Bwiti cult join in a ritual dance. Some initiates almost pass out during the many hours of visions. Others sleep for several days after the effects wear off, but ordinarily users feel little in the way of aftereffects.

Dr. Huchard used doses of 10 to 30 mg. of ibogaine in treating influenza, neurasthenia and depression, and some cardiac disorders. He found that the results were improved appetites, muscle tone and generally improved rates of recovery — along with mild euphoria.

16

Salvia Divinorum

alvia divinorum is a Mexican entheogenic plant, a species of sage. It is a member of the Labiatae or Lamiaccae family, of which mint is the most well-known member. This association is why *Salvia divinorum* is sometimes called Diviner's Mint. Other names for this tropical shrub are Divine Sage, *Ska Maria Pastora, Hojas de la Pastora* or Leaves of the Shepherdess, *Yerba de Maria* or Herb of Maria, and *Hiebra de la Virgen* or Herb of the Virgin.

Like the other heavenly highs, *Salvia* is a living marvel—"something that causes wonder or astonishment". It has a history of use in the initiation and facilitation of shamanic practice among such peoples as the Mazatec Indians of the Sierra Mazateca region of Oaxaca, Mexico, and possibly by earlier civilizations. In addition to its capacity as a tool of divination, the predominant known use of this plant—aside from general problem solving, such as finding lost objects—took place in healing ceremonies.

SALVIA
divinorum
Epling & Jateva

Scientists became aware of *Salvia divinorum* in the fall of 1962 when Maria Sabina, the curandera who introduced psilocybe mushrooms to R. Gordon Wasson, gave Albert Hofmann the plant.

Use

There are reports of early use by Panamanian Cuna Indians as an analgesia. Traditionally, this plant was used by *curanderos* of the Mazatec Indians for healing, prognostication, and precognative perception. In the West it is used as a powerful tool for meditation and the exploration of consciousness.

Salvia can be made into a tea, chewed, and smoked, with or without lacing with an extract or tincture. Each method has its pros and cons. Knowledgeable users caution: when in doubt, don't!

Tea

Mazatec shamans used it to prepare a tea from 50 to 60 leaves. Because Salvinorin A is not well-absorbed by the stomach, enormous amounts of leaves are needed to make a efficacious potion. The results from such a brew tend to be longer lasting than use by other methods.

Chewing

Traditionally, Mazatecs chewed 6-18 dried or fresh leaves slowly over a half-hour period. In the process, salvinorin is absorbed through the tissues of the mouth. Sometimes the chewed leaves are swallowed, but doing so does not increase the effect. Fresh leaves are particularly unpleasantly bitter, often causing the chewer to gag.

Chewing Quids

In this method these leaves are rolled into a ball or cylinder called a "quid," which is then chewed slowly—often adding about one every ten seconds. Between chews, the mashed leaves are kept under the tongue. After about a half an hour, juice forms in the chewer's mouth and held for a time, without spitting or swallowing. Then it is all spit out into a bowl.

Quids are made from fresh leaves or dried leaves. Westerners prefer dried leaves because they are not as bitter. It takes 2 to 8 grams of dried leaves to make a quid. Eight to 28 large whole dried leaves are placed in a small bowl of cool water for 10 minutes. After the leaves have been soaking for about 10 minutes, they are removed and excess water is squeezed out.

John W. Allen

Salvia leaf.

Then the leaves are balled up into the quid. The soaking step can be skipped, but chewing on brittle, dry leaves is unpleasant. Some people sweeten the quid with sugar, honey, or an artificial sweetener, which makes chewing it a little more pleasant.

Some people recommend using mouthwash to increase the mouth tissues' ability to absorb salvinorin A. Using a toothbrush and a mouthwash containing alcohol/menthol, such as Cool Mint Listerine, they gently brush the lining of the mouth, including the top of the tongue and under the tongue, especially to remove layers of dead cells normally present. After the brushing, they then rinse with the mouthwash for about 30 seconds, making sure to swish the mouthwash everywhere in the mouth and under the tongue.

Very little is experienced in the first 12 to 15 minutes after chewing. Full effects are usually felt within 30 minutes, when the quid is usually spit out. Effects continue for about 30 to 60 minutes, then decrease, with the whole experience seldom lasting longer than an hour and a half.

Smoking

Smoking the dried leaves is a more effective method of use, and is preferred by Western enthusiasts. This *salvia* is not smoked like tobacco. It requires high temperatures to vaporize Salvinorin A.

Sometimes dried leaves are smoked in a pipe. Ignition must be very hot to vaporize the salvinorin. Usually a flame is held just above the pipe bowl and drawn down into the leaves, as the smoker inhales the vapors deeply and quickly to get an effect. The full dose must be ingested within a two-to-three minute period because Salvinorin A is rapidly metabolized once in the body.

The leaves are generally smoked in a short-stemed tobacco pipe, in a bong, or in a "steam-roller" pipe. First effects are noticed within a minute of inhaling. After 5 to 6 minutes the effects gradually subside, with total duration of the experience generally lasting less than 30 minutes. Sometimes it can continue as long as an hour.

Extracts

Extracts, which are used in smokes and not taken orally, are a much more effective way to experience the full effects of this magical plant. Extracts are available in 5X and 10X formulations, which means that they are 5 times or 10 times stronger than plain leaf. There are two types of extracts on the market—regular and standardized. Regular extracts are made by soaking *Salvia divinorum* in a solvent to dissolve the Salvinorin A out of the leaves. The process also pulls out chlorophyll and plant fats which are dissolved in the extract and deposited into the lungs when smoked.

Standardized extract is made by first producing pure crystalline Salvinorin A, which is then applied to the leaves, so no extra chlorophyll or plant fats get into this combo. Standardized extracts burn cleanly, and are milder on the lungs because they produce smoke with less unhealthy tar in it.

Extract Doses

Additionally, standardized extract yields a guaranteed quantity of the active ingredient whereas with a regular extract the quantity is unknown. A 5X standardized extract contains 12.5 mg of Salvinorin A per gram of leaf, while 10X standardized extract has 25 mg per gram of leaf. A gram of standardized 5X contains approximately 18 moderate doses, or 12 full doses. 10X contains twice this amount.

If using the 5X, start with one or two lungfuls and wait and see where that takes you before trying more. If using the 10X, start with just one lungful, and do not use a bong when smoking the 10X as this can deliver too large a dose of this product.

Tincture

Daniel Siebert developed a *salvia* tincture which he calls "Sage Goddess Emerald Essence". This fluid extract of *Salvia divinorum* is held in the mouth until the salvinorin content has been absorbed. Siebert recommends diluting the tincture with hot water because it is quite irritating to the mouth due to the high alcohol content. With a dropper, the tincture can be a measured dose sent into a shot glass with an equal volume of heated water.

After mixing the two, the contents are sipped, and held in the mouth with the tongue elevated above the floor of the mouth to allow the sublingual tissues under the tongue to absorb the salvinorin. The fluid is kept in the mouth until the desired effect is reached, or a half hour has passed. Then it is swallowed or spit out.

The *Salvia divinorum* tincture has the same effects as in the quid method, with the advantage of being able to adjust the dosage more precisely. With the tincture, the effects come on somewhat faster, and a tincture tastes better than the bitter quid with its mushy leaves. Some people experiencing a tincture have felt a "burning" of the lining of the mouth, which occurs when the alcohol in the tincture has not been sufficiently diluted.

When this *Salvia* is consumed in tincture-form and held in the mouth, the effects come on in 10 to 15 minutes and quickly develop to a peak level that lasts 20 to 40 minutes, then gradually diminishes over an additional 30 to 60 minutes.

Effects

Salvia divinorum is a visionary herb that has been used for hundreds of years in religious and healing ceremonies by the Mazatec Indians to achieve a unique state of "devine inebriation".

The profound introspecive state of awareness this triggers is unique, promoting meditiation, contemplation, and self-reflection. *Salvia*'s effects are so intense that only a small group of people wish to repeat the experience.

On the other hand, as Daniel Siebert points out, *Salvia* has fascinating entheogenic effects, along with sensual enhancement, magical journeys, enchantment, apparent time travel, philosophical insights, spiritual experiences, and perhaps even healing and divination effects. Siebert and many others emphasize that *Salvia divinorum* is not recommended for recreational use and should not be used casually. He recommends it be only used in a thoughtful, intelligent manner by responsible adults who are of "sound mind and clear intent".

Salvia divinorum is a consciousness-changing herb that can be used in a vision quest, or in a healing ritual. In the right setting, this Salvia makes it possible to see visions. It is an herb with a long tradition of sacred use. It is useful for deep meditation. Noise and distraction interfere with the experience. It is definitely not a party drug.

Usually people report feeling clear-headed and mentally refreshed after a *Salvia divinorum* experience although some people suffer mild headaches after smoking it. Apparently the headaches result from smoke-induced sinus irritation. Like tobacco smoke, any Salvia smoke is irritating to the lungs.

Intensity Levels

Experiences range in intensity from subtle to extremely powerful. The strength of its effects depend on how much is consumed, the consumption method, and individual body chemistry. There has been recorded no fatal overdose when leaves are chewed. It is not habit forming and it seldom produces adverse side-effects, such as a hangover or "residual body load". Its use is not criminal in most countries. This *Salvia's* effects are brief in duration and the user returns to a normal conscious state rather quickly.

In his *User's Guide*, Siebert describes six levels of inebriation, beginning on the low end of the scale with subtle effects wherein the user has a feeling that "something" is happening but can not say just what. This mild level, which is characterized by relaxation and increased sensual appreciation is useful for meditation as well as facilitating sexual pleasure.

The next level in Siebert's model manifests altered perception wherein colors and textures are more pronounced and appreciation of music is enhanced. The user often experiences some space distortions, so that surroundings appear of greater or lesser depth than usual. Thinking is less ordered and more playful but rarely accompanied by visions at this level.

The middle level in Siebert's scheme is a visionary state. When eyes are closed, the user experiences so-called "eye candy" — fractal patterns, vine-like and geometric patterns, and visions of unusual objects. However, these visions are not confused with reality. This level is similar to the hypnagogic phenomena often experienced just before falling to sleep.

The next level is a vivid visionary state with complex three-dimensional scenes and, sometimes, even voices may be heard. While the user continues to have contact with reality when opening the eyes, consensus reality can be lost when eyes are closed as the user enters into a dreamlike scene. At this level users report shamanistic journeying and encounters with entities and spirits. Some users find travel to other ages may occur and they may vividly experience the life of another person. This is, as some have said, the shaman's world.

The fifth level that Siebert describes is immaterial existence, wherein the user no longer is aware of having a body. The user becomes completely involved in inner experience and a sense of individuality may be lost as one merges with "universal consciousness", or, alternatively may fuse with the consciousness of real or imagined objects. At this level it may be impossible to function. Some users

tend to try to move around, however, in this be-
fuddled state. Siebert is adament in his caution that
a sitter is necessary for safety when voyaging to
such deep levels. The user may behave in a terrifying or pleasant manner but observers often see
only a confused or disoriented person and may call
the police.

The sixth and final level is characterized by amne-
sic effects. In this deep trance state the user loses
consciousness, is lost and may be unable to recall the
experience. Injuries often can be sustained without
pain, and afterwards, users are not usually able to
remember how such an injury was created.

Dose

Pure salvinorin A is very potent. Small doses (around
a hundred micrograms) can have a noticable effect,
while a dose of 1 milligram (1/1000 of a gram) is
overwhelming for most people. For this reason, those
who are knowledgable warn that doses of pure
salvinorin A must be precisely measured.

The salvia leaf can be used more safely because it
is hundreds of times weaker than pure salvinorin A.
This salvia leaf is very gentle on the body. It is non-
toxic, and not habit-forming or addictive. There is no
record of permanent harm from overdosing. It is not
a stimulant nor is it a sedative, or a narcotic, or a
tranquilizer. In high doses it can cause visions, as is
true of many entheogens. In his book *Pharmako/
poedia*, Dale Pendell assigns *Salvia divinorum* to a
unique pharmacological class that he calls
"existentia", emphasizing the philosophical illumina-
tion that use of this plant shines on the nature of
existence itself.

Safety

Salvia divinorum is best taken in a quiet, nearly
dark room, either alone or with one or two good
friends present. It should be taken in silence or
(sometimes) with soft pleasant music playing. The
Salvia divinorum full-blown "high" seriously im-
pedes coordination, and users should never attempt
to drive or operate any machinery when under its
influence.

Always Use a Sitter

Extract-laced leaves are also smoked. Leaves laced
with extract can be very strong and should only be
smoked when a sitter is present.

Salvia divinorum should never be used in a
public environment, because doing so could draw
unwelcome attention — and even lead to the user
being arrested. Users can become so immersed in a
dream-like inner visionary state of awareness that
they completely lose touch with their surroundings
and may move around as if sleepwalking.

This is one of many reasons why it is recommended that users always have a sober sitter
present, especially when using strong doses. The
sitter's role is to prevent the user from knocking
over lit candles, dropping lit matches, falling over
furniture or running out into the street in a state
that resembles wild craziness

When smoking, it is recommended that the
smoker use a hand-held butune lighter that will go
out on its own and not a match which could ignite
something. It is a good idea to have at hand an
ashtray in which to put the pipe, because when
immersed in the experience, the smoker can forget

all about holding a lit pipe, which could drop, causing a fire. Thus, it is advised to always have a sitter present when smoking.

Vaporizing Dangers

Leaves and extract-laced leaves can be smoked in a vaporizer, which is a device that heats up material without burning it. However, vaporization can be deceiving because little smoke is produced, making it easy to inhale a large dose without meaning to do so. Commercial vaporizers made for smoking Cannabis do not work well with Salvia. Experienced smokers warn that vaporization should not be used by those new to *Salvia divinorum*. Anyone trying vaporization absolutely *must* have a sitter present.

It is recommended that Salvinorin A never be used in a vaporizer, because it can be extremely dangerous if too large of a dose is inhaled. The dose must be measured very precisely, with a chemical balance capable of weighing micrograms (millionths of a gram). Such analytical balances are expensive. However, standardized doses of Salvinorin A on leaves is available through underground herbalists. Such preparations reduce the risk of overdose by making it possible to inhale precisely-measured doses without having to have an analytical balance.

Generally speaking, it is best to avoid overly-concentrated extracts, vaporizers, and pure Salvinorin A. Chewing quid, using tincture, smoking leaves, or smoking mild-to-medium strength extracts will produce sufficiently strong effects for most people. There is no need to experiment with stronger and more dangerous ways of taking *Salvia divinorum.*

Drying

When dried *Salvia divinorum* leaves are stored in sealed containers away from light, they will retain their potency for years. Generally, the leaves are dried before storing.

Basic Drying Method

Leaves that die or are shed are gathered and placed on a plate in an area with low humidity, and turned often. It is not known if naturally shed leaves are stronger or weaker than picked leaves. The advantage of gathering fallen leaves, rather than picking growing ones, is that the plant is not deprived of the leaves that it needs.

Salvia "Tobacco"

Large freshly-picked leaves are placed one atop another, then cut through to make quarter-inch strips. These strips are then piled on a plate into a heap and turned twice daily until dry, but not crispy. The resulting "tobacco" is said to give a smoother smoke than thoroughly dried leaves. There is some speculation that this slow partial drying results in weaker leaves that may not keep as long as thoroughly dried, crispy leaves.

John Allen

Salvia Tobacco

Dehydrator

When a food dehydrator is used the drying is fast and thorough. Properly dried leaves, including the leaf stems, are crispy. The leaf stems snap when pressure is applied to them.

Oven Drying

In this method leaves are placed on an oven-proof dish and placed in an oven heated to 175 degrees Fahrenheit. The main drawback of this approach is that it may be hard to keep oven temperatures at an optimal range.

Calcium Chloride (CaC_{12}) Drying.

Calcium chloride, which can be purchased from chemical supply houses, or as "Damp-Rid" from most hardware stores, is placed in the bottom of a polyethylene container with a piece of aluminum foil over it but not touching the CaC_{12}. Salvia leaves are laid out on top of foil. The leaves should not actually touch the the CaC_{12}, which can be achieved by curling the edges of the foil up. Then the container is sealed for about two days, which is usually sufficient to thoroughly dry the leaves.

Botany

Salvia divinorum's leaves are oval-shaped and delicate, resembling those of a Coleus, sometimes yellow or yellow-green, and are often described as being irridescent. Tiny hairs, known as trichomes, cover the leaves to give them a smooth, shimmering appearance. It can grow up to 8-feet tall in tropical conditions. Plants grown in Northern climates are usually propagated by cuttings. Like many semi-tropical perennials, *Salvia divinorum* makes an attactive house plant when grown in a pot loosely filled with ultra-rich, moist soil that is well-drained.

Salvia divinorum prefers warmth and high humidity, and thrives in moderate to warm summer temperatures, especially when sprayed with a light mist of water. Frost kills *salvia divinorum.*

Chemistry

The psychoactive ingredient in *Salvia divinorum* is a chemical called salvinorin A ($C_{23}H_{28}O_8$). Salvinorins are the agents for this plant's entheogenic effects. It is considered by some to be the strongest naturally-occurring entheogenic. It is a potent, highly selective kappa-opioid receptor agonist which is not chemically related to any other psychoactive drug. Unlike most visionary compounds, it is not an alkaloid.

Legal Status

Salvia divinorum and its active principal Salvinorin A have not (yet) been outlawed in the United States or Europe. Australia has passed legislation criminalizing Salvinorin A.

17

Kava-Kava

 Kava-kava is a mild drug that has soporific and diuretic affects. It is also a muscle relaxant. As an anesthetic, it rivals cocaine. Some authorities, such as Ron Siegel, describe it as a sedative hypnotic. It produces euphoria and relaxation without impairing mental alertness. Its subtlety and complexity make it difficult to place in any of the common drug categories. Kava-kava is not illegal and is available in herb shops and through mail-order such as from those advertising in *High Times Magazine.*

Kava-kava has a strong, pleasant smell with a peppery taste that can be astringent, acrid or earthy. Detractors describe the taste as peppery, or bitter dirt. Commercial preparations often try to mask the natural taste with flavorings such as banana and vanilla.

Kava root has been a part of Polynesian culture for many hundreds of years. It is so popular that many people in the South Pacific have given up drinking alcohol after being introduced to kava-kava.

Its original range was from New Guinea to Hawaii but today kava-kava is an important entheogen in Melanesia, Polynesia, and Micronesia, and is becoming increasingly popular around the world. So much so that it is being packaged and sold commercially as a supplement and as a ready-to-use drink that can be ordered on the Internet.

Use

In Hawaii, according to Hoffer and Osmond, nobles used Kava-Kava socially for pleasure, the priests used it ceremoniously while the working class used it for relaxation. When kava-kava was given to mediums it seems to have enhanced their psychic powers. Others consume the beverage to increase inspiration and assist focused contemplation. Some investigators who have experimented with use LSD and psilocybin have employed it in this way.

Kava-kava is commonly used medically to treat headaches, sleeping disorders, relieve stress, and inhibit obesity by decreasing appetite. There is a long list of other remedial uses, including the curing of leprosy, the induction of abortion by placing kava leaves in the vagina, the curing of tuberculosis, and using it as an anesthetic during tattoo-ing. Not all of these tradi-tional uses have been scientifically validated, however.

Carved Kava-Kava bowl

Kava-Kava has a history of use in mystical rites such as to ward off sorcerers, for religious purposes, and for inspiration. It is seen as a way to communicate with gods and ancestors. For example, a song writer may go into forest that he knows to be inhabited by the ghosts of ancestors because important men are often buried in kava-drinking circles specifically for the purpose of calling their spirits in the kava trance. After eating a little food, perhaps roasting a chicken, and drinking kava-kava, the song writer lies back and listens as the kava opens his ears to ghost songs.

The cup bearer is about to present the cup in Fijian ceremony.

The affect of kava is to decrease sexual desire and response. Most of the muscle relaxation is from the waist down. That is why kava drinkers walk like a "drunk".

Effects

When drinking kava, the mouth becomes numb immediately. At first there is pleasant stimulation, followed by still mental alertness for about a half-hour with a feeling of euphoria and lethargy, after which the drinker tends to desire sleep. Large kava doses cause pupil dilation, alter perception of depth and distance, and affect balance and motor equilibrium.

All agree that kava produces a carefree and happy state with no hangover—a noticeable mental or physical excitation. According to Louis Lewin, this is "a real euphoriant which in the beginning made speech more fluent and lively and increased sensitivity to subtle sounds. The subjects were never angry, aggressive or noisy".

When large quantities are consumed, vision is disturbed, pupils are dilated and walking is difficult. The elders used to say, "If you drink too much root you must walk backwards, so the ground does not come up to greet you". Kava-kava taken regularly in large amounts has caused drinkers' legs to "become tired and weak, their muscles were controlled poorly; their gait unsteady, and they appeared to be drunk". But the mental changes are usually of a pleasant kind and, many feel, quite magical.

A surprising large number of visitors to the Polynesian Islands are said to have considered kava-kava superior to champagne. There's a sort of scaling of the skin that develops when kava-kava is used frequently and in large amounts.

Kava reduces appetite. Overeating when drinking it may induce nausea. Kava's effects last two to four hours, sometimes up to eight hours, leaving one feeling pleasant and relaxed.

Warnings

Kava-kava should not be taken within thirty-six hours of surgery because it can interfere with the anesthesia as well as prevent clotting. The physician should always be informed when a patient has been taking kava-kava or any other herb, supplement, or medicine.

An FDA (Food and Drug Administration) advisory warns that there is the potential risk of severe liver injury, including hepatitis, cirrhosis, and liver failure associated with the use of kava-containing dietary supplements. Regulatory agencies in other countries, including Germany, Switzerland, France, Canada, and the United Kingdom, have taken actions ranging from warning consumers about the potential risks of kava use to removing kava-containing products from the marketplace. Although liver damage appears to be rare, users should be informed of this potential risk. Apparently as least four patients required liver transplants.

Given these reports, persons who have liver disease or liver problems, or persons who are taking drug products that can affect the liver, should consult a physician before using kava-containing supplements.

Kavalactones can attach to skin proteins, forming allergens. Thus heavy, long-term use of kava may cause scleroderma, lesions, "alligator skin". When kava kava consumption is decreased the condition disappears.

Some believe that the plant varieties that induce the best psychoactive effect had a high percentage of kavain (K), while having a low percentage of

DHM (dihydromethysticin). Plants high in DHM tend to create nausea and long-lasting effects. Others believe that the effects of the various kavalactones are synergistic, making every kava drink a complex cocktail

Preparation

In tourist bars the roots are processed with a meat grinder. Traditional Tongan rules indicated that it is best if the preparation is done by a circumcised virgin boy or by a flower-bedecked bare-breasted virgin girl sitting cross-legged on a mat.

For five or ten minutes the fresh root is chewed to soften and separate the fibers. The mass is then spat onto leaves and the process is repeated, usually three times. Whether chewed, pounded or ground, the result is infused with cold water and filtered through anything from coconut fronds to a woman's slip, then drunk quickly so as to not taste its bitterness. The typical native serving of mild kava is one to three coconut shells full. A half of a coconut shell of strong kava—1.0 to 1.5 g of psychoactive resin—is enough to put a drinker into deep sleep within about a half hour.

Kava-kava root:
1, Irregular
piece of the root.
2, Transverse
section.
3, Large pith.

Squibb Handbook

Kava-kava's mental action is caused by at least six resinous alpha pyrones—kawain, dihydrokawain, methysticin, dihydromethysticin, yangonin and dihydroyangonin. Because these alpha pyrones are not water soluble, they must be emulsified into water or coconut milk. According to Adam Gottlieb in *Sex Drugs and Aphrodisiacs,* this is accomplished by prechewing the root as is done in the islands or by adding a little salad oil and lecithin and mixing it up in a blender. To do this, mix one ounce of powdered kava-kava, ten ounces of water, two tablespoons of coconut or olive oil and one tablespoon of lecithin granules, which are available at health food stores, in a blender until it attains a milky appearance. This amount serves two to four persons. Kava must be drunk fresh because prepared kava spoils within two days.

Botany

Kava-kava comes from the root pulp and lower stems of a tall perennial shrub called Kava (*Piper methysticum Forst. f.*), from the pepper family *Piperaceae,* which is native to the South Pacific islands. The kava plant has over a thousand other names, including 'awa, yangona, rauschpfeffer, kawa, kava pepper, intoxicating pepper, kew, tonga, sakau, tonga, and wurzelstock.

There are also distinct names for the more than fifty varieties of kava. It is related to *piper betle,* whose leaf is used to wrap betel nuts; and black pepper (*piper negrum*). The plant grows best near sea level in areas like the Solomon and Fiji Islands, Samoa, Tahiti and New Guinea, and reaches heights of twenty feet.

Kavalactones, the active principles of the plant, are concentrated in the woodstock and in the roots. Strength and potency varies greatly from plant to plant and from area to area. Young plants attains a root thickness of three to five inches within three or four years. The roots in older plants become heavy and knotted, accumulating strength and flavor.

Steinmetz: *Kava-Kava*

Kava-Kava

Cultivation

Kava is grown from stem cuttings. In the United States kava can be easily grown in a hot-house. In farming systems it needs to grow in shaded areas, protected from wind in areas of high temperature (20° to 35° C) and high humidity (70 to 100% relative humidity). Kava grows best on hillsides in deep, well-drained soils rich with organic matter and nutrients. Valley floors with poor drainage may induce root rot. Silica-clay soils with a pH of 5.5 to 6.5 are best.

Kava may also be planted in fern trees, planted around irrigated taro, cultivated in beds shaded with sago palm leaves, besides streams and at the edge of woods. According to S.H. Riesenberg's description of cultivation techniques in island communities:

...it is easy to tend; it is necessary to clean around it only once a month....The cuttings are made two joints long if the branch is more than an inch in diameter, four joints if less; they are severed diagonally, between the nodes. They are planted about one yard apart in cleaned ground prepared first with a digging stick; later they are thinned out to two or more yards; but single plants may be seen sometimes growing in a thicket of other species of plants. The cutting is stuck into the ground somewhat diago- nally to bury one node. Usually two cuttings are planted in the same spot to produce a large plant. If they cannot be planted the same day they are cut, they are bound into bundles and soaked in water by day, left in the dewy grass at night... A small [kava garden] contains a hundred plants, a large one five or six hundred. A large garden is a greater source of pride but is usually kept very secret, for fear of witchcraft which will cause the plants to dry up.

Chemistry

The active constituents of kava's chemistry—the major and minor kavalactones—were explored by Lebot and Lébesque. The major kavalactones con- stitute 96 percent of the total lipids, which Lebot and Lébesque believe are responsible for the effects of kava ingestion.

Six Major Kavalactones

Kavain (K)

Yangonin (Y)

Dihydromethysticin (DHM)

Demethoxy-yangolin (DMY)

Dihydrokavain (DHK);

Methsticin

Some believe that the plant varieties that induce the best psychoactive effect had a high percentage of kavain (K), while having a low percentage of DHM (dihydromethysticin). Plants high in DHM tend to create nausea and long-lasting effects. Others believe that the effects of the various kavalactones are synergistic, making every kava drink a complex cocktail.

18

Yohimbe

his "psychedelic stimulant" is derived primarily from the bark of a West African tree called *Pausinystalia* or *Corynanthe yohimbe*, although it is also present in other species of Corynanthe and in *Aspidosperma quebranchoblanco* and *Mitragyna stipulosa*. These tall evergreen trees grow throughout the African nations of Cameroon, southwestern Nigeria, Zaire, the Congo, and Gabon. Yohimbe trees grow as high as 90 feet and as broad as 40 feet. In South America a similar plant is called Quebracho.

Use

Yohimbe is a sensual stimulant for both men and women. It increases blood flow to the genitals and stimulates the pelvic nerve ganglia. It is known to cause firm erections in men and therefore is used in erectile-disfunction treatment (some forms of yohimbe have been approved by the FDA (United

States Food and Drug Administration) for the treatment of sexual disfunction). For centuries yohimbine bark has been used as a powerful aphrodisiac in ritual ceremonies. African tribes use it for mating rituals and rites of conception. It is also used to treat angina and hypertension. Yohimbe is smoked and snuffed by natives for it hallucinogenic effect. Some chew it to ease a cough. Others apply a dressing of ground bark to yaws (an infectious tropical skin disease) and to itching skin.

Preparation

This bark is generally prepared by boiling—so that psychoactive elements are leached out and starting material can be thrown away. A tea is brewed of six teaspoons of shaved inner bark in one pint of boiling water for ten minutes, strained, and sipped slowly one or two hours before sexual activity. Addition of 500 mg. vitamin C makes the yohimbe effect faster and stronger. Because the alkaloid taste is unpleasant a sweetener such as honey is often used.

Effects

When this alkaloid is brewed as a tea and then drunk, its effects come on within forty-five minutes to an hour. The action is reportedly swifter if taken with 500 mg. vitamin C.

Yohimbe has serotonergic, noradrenergic, and dopaminergic effects on the nervous system. Yohimbine increases noradrenergic (MHPG and VMA) and dopaminergic (HVA) cerebrospinal metabolites.

Mental effects are fairly mild. Yohimbine is a mild serotonin inhibitor. Yohimbe has slight "hallucinogenic effects" that last for about two hours. Normally there are no undesirable after affects. Some research shows that yohimbe has antioxidant effects. It also helps to prevent arteries from becoming clogged and to help prevent heart attacks.

Aphrodisiac

There is an increase in vasodilation and peripheral blood flow (lowering blood pressure), along with stimulation of the spinal ganglia, which control erectile tissue. and is believed to make erections harder and easier to maintain.

Other pleasurable effects are warm spinal shivers which are especially enjoyable during coitus and orgasm (bodies feel like they are melting into one another), psychic stimulations, mild perceptual changes without hallucinations, and heightening of emotional and sexual feeling . . .

Yohimbe will not help impotency that stems from organic nerve trouble. However, it is used in treating organic (physiological) and psychogenic (mental) forms of impotence. People with inflamed genitals should not take yohimbe.

Warning

Yohimbe increases amphetamine effects and toxicity and should not be taken with any stimulant. Overdosing is a danger. The difference between an effective dose and a toxic dose is very small. Generally a smaller dose is better until one finds its affects. Before taking any yohimbe product or extract tell your health practitioner, especially if you are taking psychiatric or cardiac medication.

Nasal decongestants and diet aids containing phe-
nylpropanolamine may also cause adverse effects.

People with high blood pressure should be
especially cautious. Because yohimbe is an MOA
inhibitor do not take it with any drinks or foods
containing high amounts of tyramine. That may
include all wines, beer and ale; yeasty products,
cheese, pepperoni, pickled herring, meat extracts,
chicken liver, salted dried fish, avocado, green bean
pods, eggplant, bouillon cubes, soya, stored beef,
figs, soy sauce, oranges, banana, red plums, bolo-
gna, salami, and raisins. Be especially careful not to
take it with the amino acids phenylalanine and
tyrosine.

Individuals with sensitive stomachs may
experience some queasiness or mild nausea
for a few minutes shortly after drinking the
tea. It is best to sip it slowly. Yohimbine
should not be used by persons suffering
from blood pressure disorders, diabetes,
hypoglycemia, or active ailments or injuries
to kidneys, liver or heart. It is a brief-acting
monoamine oxidase inhibitor (MOAI) and
should not be used by persons under the
influence of alcohol, amphetamines (even
diet pills), antihistamines, narcotics, or
certain tranquilizers (Librium is OK).
Yohimbe may cause insomnia in some persons if taken too near retiring.

—Adam Gottleib
Sex, Drugs and Aphrodisiacs

Yohimbe is a MAO-inhibitor, which alters adrenal and other metabolic functions. Avoid chocolate, cheeses, sherry, bananas, pineapples, sauerkraut and other foods containing tryptophans for 12 hours before and after use. The combination may trigger a dangerous rise in blood pressure combined with shortness of breath.

People with diabetes, kidney or heart disease should never experiment with yohimbe. Moreover, yohimbe should not be used with mescaline, LSD, MDA, MMDA or amphetamines.

Yohimbe should not be used excessively or in the long-term. Yohimbine may cause increased heart rate, frequent urination, water retention, rise in body temperature, weakness, gastrointestinal problems, hyperactivity, high blood pressure, excessive adrenal or sympathetic nerve stimulation, anxiety, headache, nausea, skin flushing, sweating, dizziness, and panic attacks.

In case of adverse reaction, the distressed person should get medical help. Yohimbe is legal, so there is no threat in seeing a doctor. Sodium amytal is the best antidote for yohimbe poisoning, which should be administered by a physician. Self-administration of barbituates during a panic is dangerous. People self-prescribing can easily overdo it.

Botany

Yohimbe is a ninety-foot tall tree with oval leaves between three and five inches long. Its names include yohimbe and yohimba. This plant is also referred to as *Pausinystalia yohimbe.*

Chemistry

The active ingredients are yohimbine and other indole alkaloids with a chemical similarity to reserpine. It is a 3alpha-15alpha-20beta-17alpha-hydroxy Yohimbine-16alpha-carboxylic acid methyl ester. It is an alpha-2 adrenergic antagonist, thus increasing adrenergic activity. The yohimbine isomer rauwolscine (or alpha-yohimbine) is also found in the East Indian Snakeroot (Rauwolfia serpentina) and it is stimulatory by inhibiting the enzyme monoamine oxidase.

Yohimbine content is approximately six percent in the shaved inner bark. Other minor alkaloids in yohimbe bark are ajmaline, corynanthine, quebrachine, tetrahydromethylcorynanthein, and alloyohimbine.

19

Nutmeg

For most of us when we hear about nutmeg we think of eggnog and jingle bells. Few people realize that, when consumed in high doses, nutmeg is a powerful mind-bender. A sprinkle of nutmeg is a delightfully bitter-cinnamon treat, but swallowing a few teaspoons can bring on an intense hallucinogenic high.

Nutmeg is the dried kernel of *Myristica fragrans*, a tree native to the Spice Islands. It contains a volatile oil includes psychotropic compounds myristicin and elemicin, which is like mescaline, another 3,4,5-trimethoxybenzene derivative. It is believed that when ingested these two compounds break down into MMDA and TMA, which are psychoactive substances.

Nutmeg is the ground up seed of an evergreen tropical tree. The fruit looks much like a peach and contains a brownish-purple, shiny kernel encased within a bright orange-red or red covering. The

Squibb Handbook

Myristica (nutmeg). 1. Penang nutmeg. 2. Round West India nutmegs. 3. Banda nutmegs. 4. Cross section. 5. Top of seed. 6. Base of seed. 7. Worry seed.

covering, or aril, is used for production of mace. The seed when dried in the sun for about two months becomes nutmeg when ground up. The flesh of the nutmeg fruit is eaten or can be preserved like candy. The nutmeg tree yields two quite separate spices. The large nutmeg seed is covered with a ruby-red membrane, called an aril, that coils around the pit. This membrane is the source of mace, another seasonal spice.

folk Medicine

Traditionally, nutmeg was valued as a cure to various ills, including the plague. The Chinese have traditionally used nutmeg to calm an upset stomach or relieve rheumatism. Southeast Asian villagers mix nutmeg seeds with cooked rice as a remedy for dysentery, anorexia and colic. Lovers have used nutmeg to boost libido.

Nutmeg appears in the Hindu Pharmacopoeia as a treatment for fever, asthma and heart disease. Early Arab physicians used it for digestive disorders, kidney disease and lymphatic ailments.

Yemeni men are said to consume nutmeg to increase and maintain sexual vigor. Researchers in the late 20th Century uncovered evidence that myristicin in nutmeg—also found in parsley and carrots—inhibits lung tumors in lab mice. Nutmeg oil was used traditionally in Afghanistan as a stimulant.

Spice of Madness

The earliest record of nutmeg's mental effects is from 1576 when a pregnant English woman became deliriously inebriated after eating ten or twelve nutmegs. She was lucky not to have died. Charles Sackville, the sixth Earl of Dorset, is reputed to have abused the spice. According to one account, he was imprisoned after an evening of nutmeg frenzy for "running naked through the street".

During the psychedelic 1960s nutmeg was rediscovered as a legal and cheap hallucinogen. There are many stories of boarding school kids and prisoners using nutmeg because they couldn't get other drugs. There are accounts that Malcolm X, the black activist, got high on nutmeg in a Boston jail. By another account Charlie Parker, the jazz musician, imbibed in nutmeg, which he washed down with soda pop.

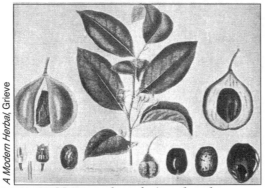

A Modern Herbal, Grieve

Nutmeg plant, fruit and seeds.

The High

Nutmeg is a psychedelic of last resort and

has sent some to the emergency room. Most people who have had an adverse reaction take too much, which leads to an unpleasant high that few want to repeat.

Nearly all accounts of nutmeg inebriation agree that it is accompanied by unpleasant somatic side-effects. Nausea is common in the first 45 minutes. Silly feelings and giggling come on several hours after ingestion, followed by dry mouth. The eyes are usually bloodshot and the skin flushed. Incoherent speech, and impaired motor function accompany heavy intoxicated feelings, followed by feeling tranquil and stupor with euphoria, disturbed sleep and twilight-state dreams.

Dose

The general dose for hallucinogenic use is 5-20 grams of whole or ground nutmeg for an experience that lasts about 12 hours, followed by drowsiness and sleep for about 24 hours. Consuming large amounts of nutmeg may cause constipation and difficulty urinating.

There is evidence that consuming large amounts of nutmeg can damage the liver with oil deposits and that the safrole in nutmeg is toxic to the liver. Adam Gottlieb in *Legal Highs* says that it is not recommended as a hallucinogen.

Afterword by Susan Blackmore
The intoxication instinct

rom alcohol and cannabis to cocaine and LSD, it seems there are no limits to our appetite for mind-altering substances. What is it about human nature that drives us to get out of our heads, ask Helen Phillips and Graham Lawton

In the Smoke Shack, a "head shop" in Nelson, British Columbia, the air is thick with marijuana and the atmosphere is mellow as the staff stage a demo of their dope-related paraphernalia. The clients range from tourists and business types to the dreadlocked and dishevelled. All walks of life are welcome.

Over the border in the US, the police call to the man in the car for the last time. If he doesn't step out they will shoot. He stays put—maybe because he's embarrassed about being caught naked from the waist down, clearly aroused. Or maybe he's just too high on methamphetamine to care.

High up in the mountains of Peru the men brew coca leaves into a tea. While they don't approve of the habit of snorting the powdered extract, the tea gives them a mild buzz that helps fight the headaches and nausea of altitude sickness. Up here, cocaine is part of life.

Lounging in a restaurant, two old friends share a second bottle of wine, sinking lower in their seats as they enjoy the numbing haze and warmth it creates. Later they'll order brandy. The bartender pours himself a cup of coffee. It's going to be a long shift.

Pursuit of Intoxication

As diverse as these episodes are, there is a clear common thread running through them: the pursuit of intoxication. Since prehistoric times, humans have been seeking out and using intoxicating substances. Most people who have ever lived have experienced a chemically induced altered state of consciousness, and the same is true of people alive today.

That's not to say that everybody is constantly fighting the urge to get high, nor that intoxication is somehow a normal state of consciousness. But how many of us can claim never to have experienced an altered state, whether it be a caffeine kick to help us get going in the morning, a relaxing beer after work, a few puffs on a joint at a party or the euphoric high of ecstasy?

In the present prohibitionist climate it is difficult to talk about the use of psychoactive, literally "mind-altering", substances without focusing on their harmful and habit-forming properties. And it's true that excessive use of consciousness-altering drugs, both legal and illegal, is bad for individuals and bad for society. People who seek intoxication are taking risks with their health and flirting with addiction. Drugs can lead to crime, violence, accidents, family disintegration and social decay.

Universal

Nonetheless, intoxicants remain a part of most people's lives. And indeed most of us are able to consume them in moderation without spiralling into abuse and addiction. Take alcohol, for example. Its potent psychoactive properties and potential for wreaking havoc are well known, yet the majority of people still drink and enjoy it without becoming alcoholics. There's also ample evidence that, despite public health campaigns and the threat of severe penalties, millions of people every year join the legions who have experimented with illegal substances, from cannabis and cocaine to ecstasy, amphetamines and LSD.

It seems that intoxication in one form or another is universal, a part of who we are. "It's a natural part of consciousness to change one's consciousness," argues Rick Doblin, who runs the not-for-profit Multidisciplinary Association for Psychedelic Studies in Sarasota, Florida. But why is it that we choose to alter our state of consciousness by dosing our brains with chemicals?

Why? Because we Like It

The answer is straightforward. We seek intoxication for a simple reason that we are almost too scared to admit—we like it. Intoxication can be fun, sociable, memorable, therapeutic, even mind-expanding. Saying as much in the present climate is not easy, but an increasing number of researchers now argue that unless we're prepared to look beyond the "drug problem" and acknowledge the positive aspects of intoxication, we are only seeing half the story—like researching sex while pretending it isn't fun.

Quest to Understand

A full understanding of intoxication, and the quest to achieve it, could have numerous pay-offs. For one thing there is the prospect of better ways to tackle abuse and addiction. There are also good reasons for studying intoxication as a phenomenon in its own right. What is it about psychoactive substances that we like? What do they tell us about who we are? Is there a way to get the good without the bad? Some researchers believe that such enquiries will lead to a new understanding of the human mind, including the mysteries of consciousness, or new treatments for mental illness. Others go as far as to argue that it is time for society to accept that intoxication is an inextricable part of human nature, and find a way to let us explore it openly.

The quest to understand intoxication wasn't always so constrained. Back in the 1950s, 60s and early 70s, many scientists took a very personal interest in it. In those more liberal days, researchers such as physician Andrew Weil, latterly of the National Institute for Mental Health in Maryland, and ethnobotanist Terence McKenna charted the effects of many drugs, tested them in the lab and in the field, explored their mind-altering qualities first-hand, documented their use in different cultures, and suggested that many of the compounds had medicinal benefits.

Many of these pioneering researchers came to the conclusion that seeking intoxication was programmed into human nature. As Weil pointed out in *The Natural Mind,* from an early age children experiment with spinning around or hyper-ventilating to experience mind-altering giddiness. He suggested that when we get older, this quest to alter our feelings stays with us but we pursue it chemically as well as physically.

Research Squelched

The spirit of personal research, however, was largely quashed in the late 70s and 80s as a US-led "war on drugs" took hold. Drug research became dominated by the "addiction paradigm", with pleasure and benefits strictly off-limits. "It was so controversial it had to be shut down altogether," says Charles Grob, director of the child and adolescent psychiatry department at Harbor-UCLA Medical Center in Torrance, California, whose interests lie with the potential medical use of psychedelics.

But some researchers carried on regardless. Ronald Siegel, now a psychopharmacologist at the University of California, Los Angeles, was one of them. As a psychology graduate student in the 60s he busied himself with studying pigeon memory. One day, a fellow student was arrested for marijuana possession, and his lawyer asked Siegel what he knew about the drug's effects. Not much, as it happened, so he brewed up an extract and watched what happened when a pigeon got stoned.

Ever since, he has been fascinated by intoxication, what it is and why we and other animals seek it. He managed to keep studying "controlled substances" such as LSD, mescaline, PCP, cocaine and psilocybin in his clinic, in animals and in volunteers, all legal and above board. He's passed out, thrown up, been attacked by intoxicated animals, and even been shot at by drugs barons—all in the name of research. And he has gained a unique perspective, spelled out in *Intoxication: Life in pursuit of artificial paradise,* which is being reissued next April by Park Street Press of Rochester, Vermont.

Biological Drive

Siegel believes there is a strong biological drive to seek intoxication. "It's the fourth drive," he says. "After hunger, thirst and sex, there is intoxication." Whether we are seeking pleasure, stimulation, pain relief or escape, at the root of this drive, he says, is the motivation to feel "different from normal"—what has sometimes been called "a holiday from reality". Some people reach this state through travel, books, art, roller coasters, sport, religion, exploration, love, social contact or power. Others use intoxicants. "It's the same motivation," says Siegel. "We wouldn't live if we didn't seek to feel different."

One of the main "different" feelings we want to experience is pleasure. Pleasure, neuroscientists believe, is the brain's way of telling us that we are doing something that is good for survival, such as eating and sex. The circuits that create the feeling are driven by natural opioids and cannabinoids. No surprise, then, that we have a penchant for putting versions of these chemicals into our brains.

But the equation is not quite as simple as chemical in, pleasure out. At last month's Society for Neuroscience meeting in San Diego, California, neuroscientist Kent Berridge of the University of Michigan in Ann Arbor described preliminary work showing that rats given a natural cannabinoid, anandamide, seemed to become unusually partial to sweet tastes. Rats primed with anandamide had higher pleasure responses to sugar than unprimed rats. It seems that the cannabinoid may not just be pleasurable in its own right, but also enhances other pleasurable experiences, making the world seem a generally more likeable place. Perhaps this is one aspect of the well-known "munchies" effect of marijuana, they conclude.

A related idea is that some people take psycho-active substances to suppress "negative pleasure". George Koob, a neuroscientist and addiction specialist at the Scripps Research Institute in La Jolla, California, has proposed that the brain has a natural system for limiting the amount of pleasure we can feel. He argues that pleasure has to be transient or humans and other animals would get so absorbed in it that they would succumb to the next predator that came along. Koob thinks that the brain has a way of bringing us down—a kind of "anti-pleasure" mechanism if you like. What if this system goes into overdrive? "Some people seek excessive pleasure because they are born with too much anti-pleasure," he says. "They may take drugs to feel normal."

But there is more to intoxication than simply massaging our pleasure circuits. Some altered states, Siegel believes, have a utilitarian value. Just as many animals naturally seek medicinal plants such as antibiotics or emetics, we seek to medicate our minds. When we are agitated or in pain, emotionally as well as physically, we seek substances that tranquillize and sedate. When tired or depressed, we seek stimulants. According to some researchers, including Grob, this medicinal use is an underlying thread running through all forms of intoxication.

Medicate Mood

The drive to medicate mood is pervasive throughout the animal kingdom, Siegel says, and he and his colleagues have documented thousands of examples. Elephants, for instance, enjoy the taste of fermented fruit. They will usually just browse it, but if they lose their mate (elephants usually mate for life) they may seek oblivion in an alcoholic fruit binge, even drinking neat ethanol if researchers provide it. It's hard not to conclude that, like humans, they are drowning their sorrows. Stress can also lead animals to take intoxicants as a form of escape. When stressed by overcrowding, elephants are more motivated to seek alcohol. And fear can take its toll too. During the Vietnam war, Siegel and his team filmed water buffalo grazing on opium poppies to the point of addiction. And animals don't just take downers: there are numerous reports of goats guzzling stimulants such as coffee beans and the herbal amphetamine khat.

Medication with uppers and downers may be fairly easy to understand, but there are other intoxicants whose attractions are harder to fathom. These are the hallucinogens, which can't easily be explained in purely survivalist terms. Most animals actively avoid this category of intoxicant.

Promotes Mental Health

Despite this, some researchers believe that psychedelics can have a medicinal effect in humans. Doblin, for example, argues that the drastically altered states they induce can play a role in maintaining mental health. Hallucinogens—and to some extent cannabis and MDMA—allow us to escape, temporarily, from a reality ruled by logic, ego and time, and explore other aspects of our consciousness. "The brain functions best when it has access to altered states," he says.

This might sound like hippy mumbo-jumbo, but there is plenty of evidence in the medical literature that hallucinogens are effective against mental illness, including anxiety, post-traumatic stress disorder, alcoholism and heroin addiction. Most of this research was done in the 1950s, but the field is now showing signs of a revival. Grob recently received approval to test psilocybin as a treatment for severe anxiety in terminally ill cancer patients, and there are ongoing studies in the use of psilocybin for otherwise untreatable cases of obsessive compulsive disorder, and MDMA for serious post-traumatic stress disorder.

Monkeys Get High

Medicinal properties notwithstanding, there are other ideas to explain why people take psychedelics. Siegel found that he could persuade monkeys to voluntarily smoke the hallucinogen DMT when they were in a situation of severe sensory deprivation. He had already trained three rhesus monkeys to smoke for a reward, to study the effects of nicotine. When he laced their smoking tubes with DMT, they briefly tried it, then avoided it. But after several days in darkness, with no stimulation, the monkeys began to smoke DMT voluntarily. They ended up grasping at and chasing non-existent objects and hiding from invisible dangers. "This was the first demonstration of a non-human primate voluntarily taking a hallucinogenic drug," Siegel says. "We share the same motivation to light up our lives with chemical glimpses of another world." Boredom it seems, will drive animals to experiment, even when the experience is not altogether pleasurable.

Seek Novelty

The same drive to seek novelty or stave off boredom could explain why people take drugs that have overwhelmingly negative effects. PCP, for example, which some consider to be the most dangerous illegal drug, is a "dissociative" Among its myriad effects are numbness, loss of coordination, paranoia, hallucinations, acute anxiety, mood swings and psychosis. But for some people the altered state is clearly worth it—PCP was hugely popular in the US in the 1970s. "People seem to say they liked feeling different or funny," says Siegel. "When there's nothing else to do, people will take anything to feel different."

In some ways novelty-seeking is a basic behavioural drive. Literature on child development reveals that once infants are no longer sleepy, hungry or thirsty, they will explore and seek new experiences. They wriggle their limbs, put things in their mouths, touch things, taste things and bash things together. Without this drive, they wouldn't

learn anything about the world around them. Perhaps this spirit of exploration simply continues into
adulthood in a different form.

Risk-Taking

There's another drive, too, that probably plays a
role: risk-taking. For some people taking risks is
itself pleasurable. According to Koob this might
come from a slightly different brain system to the
pleasure circuits. For animals that forage, there is
always the risk of being attacked by a predator. In
other words there is a conflict between seeking
new foraging sites, or novelty, and risk. Evolution
has got around this conundrum by making novelty
rewarding and pleasurable in its own right.

Pleasure, excitement, therapy, novelty: seen in
this light, the pursuit of intoxication looks very
different from its standard portrayal as a patho-
logical drive that must be suppressed before it
leads to harm, addiction and squalor. Yet the main-
stream debate on drugs, alcohol and tobacco
seems unable to acknowledge that there is anything positive at all to say about intoxication.
Instead it is locked into a sterile argument between
prohibitionists and those who want to reduce the
harmful effects by, for example, making heroin
available on prescription. Both groups start from
the belief that psychoactive substances are inher-
ently harmful but disagree on what to do about it.

Cognative Liberty

Some activists, however, are starting to argue for
an entirely different attitude to intoxication. One
prominent critic of the debate is Richard Glen
Boire, director of the Center for Cognitive Liberty

and Ethics in Davis, California and author of *Marijuana Law* and *Sacred Mushrooms and the Law*. He believes that intoxication is not just a part of human nature, it is a basic human right. "Why should it be illegal to alter your style of thinking?" he says. "As long as you don't do any harm to anyone else, what you do in your own mind is as private as what you do in your own bedroom." Boire advocates changes to the law that would allow people to experiment with psychoactive substances at home or in designated public places. "It's the right of people to explore the full range of consciousness, and our duty as a society to accommodate that," he says.

Risk Reduction

Some scientists are moving in the same direction, arguing that instead of suppressing, medicalising and criminalising our basic drive to experience altered states we should apply ourselves to making it safer, healthier and less squalid—in short, to taking the "toxic" out of intoxication.

The approach favoured by Siegel is to tweak existing drugs to make them better, with shorter effects and no addictive potential. "What it would be like," he says, "if we had a drug like alcohol, which didn't lead to violence, fetal damage, liver failure, that was safe, wouldn't lead to drink driving and never gave you a hangover. What would be wrong with it medically? Maybe we'd even prescribe this alcohol substitute to help people relax." We could even design entirely new chemicals that allow us to experience all the pleasures, thrills and adventures of intoxication without the downsides.

"This is not science fiction," says Siegel. "Civilisation will eventually take this direction."

Perhaps this would be the greatest contribution a full understanding of the intoxication instinct could offer—a spur for society to move beyond the irrational position of sanctioning caffeine, alcohol and tobacco while fighting a "war" against other psychoactive substances. David Lenson, a social theorist at the University of Massachusetts in Amhurst and author of *On Drugs*, makes this point by comparing the war on drugs with efforts to eradicate homosexuality: both are based on an incomplete understanding of human nature. Siegel, too, sees an analogy with sex. "We can't be expected to solve the AIDS problem by outlawing sex," he says. "We have to make drugs safe and healthy, because people are not going to be able to say no."

A Window to the Mind

Drugs provide some of the best evidence we have that the mind is the brain; that our thoughts, beliefs and perceptions are created by chemistry. Take a drug, particularly a hallucinogen, and any of these can change. This means these drugs can be scary and need to be taken with great care and respect. But it also means they have the potential to reveal some of the deepest secrets about our minds and consciousness.

A century ago, psychologist William James experimented with the anaesthetic nitrous oxide. Our normal rational consciousness, he said, is just one special type of consciousness, while all around it, "parted from it by the filmiest of screens", are other entirely different forms of consciousness, always available if the requisite stimulus is applied.

Others meticulously described the effects of inhaling ether, chloroform and cannabis, and the strange distortions of time, perception and sense of humour they induced. More curiously, they also described changes in belief, and even in philosophy. When Humphry Davy took nitrous oxide in 1799 he ended up exclaiming that "nothing exists but thoughts". Others made similar observations and found their views profoundly shifted by even brief forays to the other side of that filmy screen.

Sense of Self

This raises the peculiar question of whether what James called "our normal rational consciousness" is necessarily the best state for understanding the world. After all, if one's view of the world can change so dramatically with the aid of a simple molecule, how can we be sure that our normal brain chemistry is the one most suited to doing science and philosophy? What if our brain chemistry evolved to help us survive at the cost of giving us false beliefs about the world? If so, it is possible that mind-altering drugs might in fact give us a better, not worse, insight than we have in our so-called normal state.

Take the common hallucinogenic experience of losing our separate self, or becoming one with the universe. This may seem, to some, like mystical hogwash, but in fact it fits far better with a scientific understanding of the world than our normal dualist view. Most of us feel, most of the time, that we are some kind of separate self who inhabits our body like a driver in a car or a pilot in a plane. Throughout history many people have believed in a soul or spirit. Yet science has long known that this cannot be so. There is just a brain that is made of exactly the same kind of stuff as the world around it. We really are one with the universe.

This means that the psychedelic sense of self may actually be truer than the dualist view. So although our normal state is better for surviving and reproducing, it may not always be best for understanding who and what we are. Perhaps we ought to try doing science in some of these intoxicated states.

This was just what psychologist Charles Tart of the University of California, Davis, suggested in the journal *Science*. He likened different states of consciousness to different paradigms in science and proposed creating "state specific sciences", new sciences which would be done by scientists working and communicating in altered states. These new sciences might only have limited application but this makes the point that our normal state may not be the only way to try to understand the universe.

Since Tart's work, most psychedelic drugs have become prohibited and research has largely been stifled. Perhaps one day, when prohibition is abandoned, scientists may once again take up the promise offered by those tiny little chemicals that can tell us who and what we are.

Reprinted by permission from *New Scientist* vol. 184, issue 2473, 13 November 2004, page 32.

Ronin Books for Independent Minds